CW01082497

THE WIEAMBILLA SHOOTINGS

The true story of a long-prepared ambush by religiously motivated conspiracy theorists

JOHN KERR

Published by:
Wilkinson Publishing Pty Ltd
ACN 006 042 173
PO Box 24135
Melbourne, Vic 3001
Ph: 03 9654 5446

enquiries@wilkinsonpublishing.com.au
www.wilkinsonpublishing.com.au

Title: The Wieambilla Shootings

ISBN: 9781922810847

A catalogue record of this book is available from the National Library of Australia.

Photography credits: Front cover background photo of police tape across the road leading into Wains Road at Wieambilla, 13 December 2022 courtesy of David Clark/Newswire/Newspix. All other photographs are from the public domain.

Design by Spike Creative Pty Ltd
Ph: (03) 9427 9500
spikecreative.com.au
Printed and bound in Australia by Ligare Book Printers.

To the memory of

Rachel, Matthew and Alan

Contents

Introduction

As a nation, we need to reflect on why some teenagers are hanging Nazi flags and portraits of the Christchurch killer on their bedroom walls and why others are sharing beheading videos.
– Mike Burgess, Director-General,
Australian Security Intelligence Organisation,
Annual Threat Assessment, February 2022

The cruel, stupid, almost arbitrary shooting murders and attempted murders in Wieambilla Queensland on 12 December 2022 alerted Australians to a new threat to life, limb and the peace.

We braced ourselves for the sick work of Islamic jihadists after the 9/11 attacks on New York and Washington 20 years ago. While we were not spared that entirely, we got off light. The Islamic State caliphate in Iran and Syria was rolled back in the 2010s. Jemaah Islamiyah cells in Indonesia were suppressed by police actions and arrests at the end of that decade. The threat of ideological, political and religious violence at home seemed to have receded. The Wieambilla killings have changed all that.

* * *

When a radicalised Australian white-supremacist idiot shot and killed 51 people attending Friday prayers in mosques in Christchurch, New

Zealand on 15 March 2019 Australian law enforcement began taking a hard look – many would add an 'overdue look', as New Zealand Royal Commission found was the case among law enforcement and intelligence communities in that country – at far-right conspiracy theorists and the threat posed by so-called 'lone wolf' killers. However, it had seemed our home-grown racist nutters were content to daub a few swastikas on synagogue walls and anti-Islamic slogans on those of mosques. Ugly but not lethal acts.

Then, on 19 January 2020, a coronavirus flew in from China. A pandemic was declared. Governments, advised by health experts, worked to try to minimise the inevitable number of the corpses that followed. The public health measures, vaccination programs in particular, lockdowns, border closures and mask rules that followed were opposed with unexpected and, yes, unprecedented ferocity by tens of thousands of Australians. Pandemic drew them out, onto the street, loud, proud, and deaf to reason. Over 2020, 2021 and early 2022 street protests – sit-ins, 'Freedom Day' marches, convoys – saw scores of state police in capital cities injured.

In Melbourne, lockdown central, police used tear gas and rubber bullets to clear road and pedestrian ways. Tossing tear gas canisters and firing rubber bullets at citizens is a decision not undertaken lightly, to put it mildly. Victoria Police had not faced such a violent protest for '20 years'. It is in the nature of police media units to up-play protestor violence, and to exaggerate police injuries, but the demos in Melbourne in September and November 2021 saw three cops hospitalised for broken bones. Journalists, another tribe anti-vaxxers despised, were assaulted too, and sprayed with urine. Gallows mock-ups were paraded and shouts of 'Kill Daniel Andrews', Victoria's premier, echoed around Parliament House.[1]

The Convoy to Canberra, following a model that had converged on Canada's Ottawa, hit the federal capital in early 2022. The attack on the

US Capitol in Washington was 10 months old then.

The Australian Convoy's initial demand was for the retraction of Covid-19 rules, but the vibe at the showground and parks campsites took on many characteristics of 'a music festival'.[2] Kristy Milligan, ex-cop, terrorism scholar and XRW (eXtreme Right-Wing) tracker, noted the Red Ensign flags loved by SovCits as part of their peculiar respect for maritime/Admiralty law over that of the state, and some MAGA (Make America Great Again) caps and other Trump merchandise. She tracked too, the push for various agendas, noting the wide divisions in the ASM, an acronym for Anti-Social Movement I suspect she invented as a cover all for the diverse and inchoate beefs, frustrations and aims of those convoyed. By public address systems and bull horn, attempts for unified leadership dwindled and chaotic idiosyncratic squabbles proliferated.

The Convoy raised $160,000 via GoFundMe, and predicted ½ million people would attend. Police and media counted heads and thought about 10,000 people did. That thousands of Australians left home and hearth to demonstrate against public-health measures is remarkable. For every attendee, there were scores, perhaps hundreds, of sympathisers who stayed home.

Arrests were made. One of the ASM arrested was a doomsday prepper found with a loaded firearm, ammunition and a map of Parliament House. A man drove a truck through a barricade, and police had to smash his window to get him out; sounds like a Sovereign Citizen, as we will see. A woman in her sixties was assaulted by a protester; in court, the alleged perpetrator facing charges of inflicting grievous bodily harm, sought to defend himself with a standard SovCit legalese snow job.

Some protesters burnt the doors and entrance to Old Parliament House. The put-things-right bill was estimated to be 3.5 million taxpayer dollars.

The Canberra demonstration (and a steep bill for damage) was echoed in February for three weeks occupation on the lawns and streets around Wellington's Beehive parliament building in New Zealand. The occupiers were only cleared after a major police operation ejected them and firies put out the bonfires of their tents and playground equipment that they made.

Nor was it confined to capital cities; small cities saw home-grown local demonstrations.

Who were these angry people?

The list is long and the connections between them incoherent. Neo-nazis mingled with indigenous sovereign-land proponents. 5G conspiracy theorists – the they're-gonna-microchip-your-brain mob – joined arms with ultra-religious Christian groups. The United Australia Party, a registered *bona fide* political group, and the far-right Proud Boys, a borrowing from Trump's America, listened to speeches from an ex-Liberal Party politician. Sovereign Citizens showed up. Milligan called it 'a salad bar'. If there was one thing – perhaps the only thing – they agreed on, it was that vaccination was a bad thing.

That these angry souls even existed at all may very well have been because their predecessors were inoculated against smallpox, measles, mumps, rubella, polio and so on. This probability was lost in their noise. Their passion admitted no logic, science or balance. Old people remembered the empty desk at school because So-and-so had 'got the polio' and was paralysed, fighting for his or her life in the dreaded iron lung of the 1950s, remembered the relief when Dr Salk's oral vaccine became available, remembered the triumph as the vaccine rolled the polio virus almost from the face of the planet.

* * *

After the events of 12 December 2022 in Wieambilla previous police-dissident interactions in the US cannot be ignored. Whether the three Trains knew it or not, and there is no record they did, a lot of the online conspiracy theorists they followed were heavily influenced by events there.

One narrative thread of what follows here is the way three people – Nathaniel, Stacey and especially Gareth Train – managed to so demonise the state and the law enforcement officers who embodied it for them that they awarded themselves the bogus moral up-tick they needed to murder anonymous people. Gareth Train referred to people who did not agree with his shallow, hate-driven view of the world's flesh-and-blood humanity as 'soulless, spiritless meat suits'.

I believe the killers died smug, feeling righteous and even heroic; the psychology of how they managed to create that sick mind-set is not clear to me, but their descent into heartless violence and essentially suicide is charted wherever they left a mark. Least there be the slightest doubt, the killings of Rachael, Matthew and Alan, as I and I suspect a lot of people now think of the victims, was a vile act, one without a redeeming or mitigating factor I could find or suggest, heartbreaking as well as mind-blowingly contemptible.

Queensland Police will reveal the results of their investigations to the State Coroner, Mr Terry Ryan SM, with Ruth O'Gorman KC as counsel-assisting, in Brisbane at some stage in late 2023. His inquest will examine all six deaths after a second pre-inquest conference planned for early 2024 – these are used to handle court housework as a rule – and with hearings to follow. Those hearings will examine at least 152 statements, mostly prepared by Ethical Standards police, of witnesses, psychologists, counter-terrorism experts; 325 exhibits including six years of Train phone records, Stacey Train's diaries, victim-witness Alan's phone, and police video footage from body cams, helicopters and armoured vehicles.[3]

In the meantime, we can expect the police service to be tight lipped, as has characterised their policy and demeanour before and since they assured the public the perpetrators were an autonomous cell, that no other religiously-motivated extremist terrorists were associated with them, and that no threat to the public from there remained.

Here is what is known…

1 Sarah Krasnostein, 'The Train Family Murders', *The Monthly*, May 2023

2 'The Anti-Social Movement: the 2022 Convoy to Canberra and the Freedom Movement', Periscope, December 2022

3 Alex Brewster, *MC News* 13 January 2023; Ben Smee, *Guardian Australia*, 15 June 2023; Yahoo News 15 June 2023; *Country Caller* 16 June 2023; & others

1
The Welfare Check

You attempt to abduct us using contractors. You attempt to intimidate and target us with your Raytheon Learjets and planes. You sent 'covert' assets out here to my place in the bush. So what is your play here? To have me and my wife murdered during a state police 'welfare check'? You already tried that one.
– YouTube post on account name Mrs Yugi girawil, 12 December 2022

When police make a welfare check, a routine job for city and country cops alike, what usually happens is that officers knock on doors, or press a buzzer or intercom. In the country, particularly on isolated rural properties, they may sound a car horn or walk about the outbuildings and holler a bit to get the attention of one or more of the residents. If no-one's home, the usual thing is for an officer to leave his or her card, and write a note asking the key resident to get in touch with whoever is on the police department paperwork. If someone is home, one officer generally starts with an 'are you So-and-so?' or 'when did you last see?' type of question. The information gathered is recorded in their notepad or on their phone recorder app. They may ask the resident to show some photo identification. Then the rest of the job is done back at the station, where the file is updated and circulated to police involved.

Four on-duty Queensland Police Service constables in two vehicles drove to an isolated bush block, 251 Wains Road, Wieambilla, Queensland about 4.30 on Monday afternoon 12 December 2022, to make a welfare check. They may too have had an arrest warrant to serve on the missing man too, as we will see.

The estranged second wife of Nathaniel Charles Train in New South Wales had had no contact from him for over two months. He had uncharacteristically gone incommunicado; he was a recovering invalid; his behaviour had become odd; she was worried about him. She contacted local police. They had mechanisms for worries like this. A NSW Police Service missing-person file was created. Queensland Police were copied in because Nathaniel's brother, Gareth Train, lived on the Wieambilla block, and he may have known something useful regarding his brother's whereabouts. According to the Queensland Coroner's Court, NSW Police may also have contacted the Chinchilla Police Station specifically requesting paying 251 Wains Road a visit.

Nearly 30 people a day go missing in NSW alone. Most are quickly found and welfare checks find most of them.

A missing person file request is not the only origin of a welfare check. This author had an elderly friend living in a small country town who, uncharacteristically, was not responding to phone calls or emails. On my visits from the city to see him, we had laughed about how he had look down to see if he was barefoot or in his socks or was wearing shoes, his peripheral neuropathy having deadened feeling in his feet. Sufferers cannot, for example, climb ladders safely but that does not mean they will not give it a go. And fall off. Worried, I rang the local one-man police station. The officer said he was just going out to walk his dog, so he would call in. I said there was a dog on my friends' premises. He said, 'Betsy and my bitch get along OK, no worries.' Within an hour, the cop had rung back to say all was sweet. In his log, a welfare check.

Garry Disher's fictional Constable Paul (Hirsch) Hirschhausen of the one-officer Tiverton Station in 'wheat and wool country' in remote South Australia is a cop with a big beat. Readers of these well-researched thrillers will be aware of Hirsch's regular weekly round trips, 'patrols' he calls them, calling on the isolated, the vulnerable, those at-risk of re-offending, the frail or mentally ill, dysfunctional families and the odd eccentric day-glo crazy camped out. Regular welfare checks.

* * *

What the four cops faced at the Wains Road gate at 251 is not known outside a group of tight-lipped insiders who heard it from the survivors.

Like quite a few others on the Wieambilla blocks, Gareth Train valued privacy. At 251 Wains Road the four passed a 'No Trespassing' sign. If the gate was unlocked, that itself may have sinister implications. What we do know is that the homestead was not visible from Wains Road, that trees held security cameras and mirrors in place covering the approach, and that the inhabitants knew the cops were coming.

The two constables from the Tara Police District seem to have led the way, the two from Chinchilla falling in behind. They drove up the long driveway. They pulled up at the gate of the fenced-off homestead-and-sheds area. One of them honked the horn, a practical thing to do, a courtesy.

That four police should attend a welfare check has raised suspicions. Even a retired Northern Territory and Australian Federal Police cop of my acquaintance queried it in conversation. But such calls are also opportunities to familiarise colleagues new to the area with the roads, point out tricky spots, highlight navigation landmarks, and acquaint them of addresses with 'history', places with residents with repeat offences on their record or a reputation for violence or heavy alcohol or methamphetamine use. These four, none of them old hands, had a rookie just eight weeks on 'The Job' among them. Also, while the Wieambilla blocks lie within the Tara Police District, they border the Chinchilla one and districts cooperate. Police services are never lavish with staffing, so if, say, Chinchilla's officers are tied up and get a call that perhaps Tara can do… and vice versa.

The two Toyota LandCruiser Prado hatchbacks stopped in front of the house area's fence. The four cops got out.

The homestead gate at 251 was locked. No worries. Tara Constables Matthew Arnold and Rachael McCrow, and Chinchilla Constables Randall Kirk and Keely Bough all climbed over the fence and began to walk up to the silent house. Nobody appeared from within it, as the police's body cams attest. The four would have been in clear view to anybody in the house or in the hides and foxholes covered with scrub around it.

I cannot be sure, but it seems that no-one was in the house. The three residents – Gareth, Stacey and Nathaniel Train, or at least two of them – were in the long-prepared sniper beds outside, the kill zone long planned, dressed to kill in camouflage gear; they had either had time to dress for the ambush or had dressed like this every day in the general expectation of a visit.

Gunshots rang out. In the hail of bullets fired Matthew and Rachel were felled instantly. They did not have a chance.

When I started this book, I wrote 'Hopefully, they died instantly.' I hoped the bullets that first felled them, killed them; that they went from unsuspecting daily-routine consciousness, to shock, momentary confusion, unconsciousness, and a quick death. My hopes may have been the fate of Matthew, who was said to have been shot in the midriff, perhaps halfway over the fence, but Rachel was hit in the leg. Randall took a wound in his leg too but was able to walk.

Randall was able to get to the cab of the Chinchilla police car. Bullets smashed through the windows. He kept low, and hit the ignition. Bullets continued to smash into the van, showering him in glass shards. His impending escape seems to have attracted all the shooters' attention, diverting it from Keely. He was able to drive out of the line of fire and get to a place where he could make contact with station police. It is not clear, but it seems a mobile phone connection may have been necessary. Connection in the area is not good.

Keely Brough was not hit. She too ran from the area in front of the gate, but she found no cover. That may have saved her life. She dived into the long grass and stringy, thin open brigalow and gidgee scrub that grew at the side of the driveway, praying no bullet – and plenty of them were flying – would find her body. She crawled into the dirt, and hid. She rang 000, may have got through. She perhaps radio-ed colleagues. These communication questions remain open. But she kept her body cam running.

Two Train shooters walked up to where Matthew Arnold had fallen. They took his Glock sidearm and shot him in the head with it, very probably and hopefully, a post-mortem insult on a dead man. They took his two-way radio too. Reports of what happened next are confused and unreliable. However, it is my melancholy duty to write that some have reported that Rachel had made or was making a tourniquet to stem blood loss from her leg wound as she pleaded for her life, that she was killed by an execution-style bullet to her head from Matthew's Glock. If so, the cruelty of the Trains is made more terrible. If so, Rachael died not only in pain, but in terror.

No more than 10 minutes had passed since the four entered the property. That is a small mercy but a mercy, is it not? That the ordeal was short-lived?

The Trains, gun nuts, took Rachel's service handgun and her two-way radio too. We must await testimony from Keely Brough in the Coroner's Court to know more about this.

Meanwhile, we know she was wriggling in the dirt and grass at 251 in mortal terror. That terror is beyond any terror I, and I imagine most readers, have faced.

The shooters exited the homestead area. They set fire to the grass where Keely had last been seen upright. Clearly, they intended to flush her out and kill her. She was a prey animal then. The shooters torched the parked police vehicle. She tapped out text messages to family, as those who hunted her watched and waited: '... my time... be shot or burned alive'.

* * *

251 Wains Road

We know little about what was going down at the Tara and Chinchilla Police Stations, or the equidistant Miles one. My guess would be that vehicles idling at the station doors were filling with cops who had broken out long arms, first-aid kits, body-armour vests, anything that might be useful. We do know they hot footed it to 251 Wains Road.

We do know what was done in Brisbane. Polair helicopters took off to take a look-see over the kill site. The Special Emergency Response Team (SERT) officers – Queensland Police's SWAT team – hit the road to the same place.

Queensland Police declared a wide area around 251 Wains Road was a PSPA area under the Public Safety Preservation Act. Residents must stay indoors. Pedestrians and motorists must avoid it.

At the Miles Police Station, one cop, Con Scott Pogan, wore two hats, one blue of course and an orange one. He was the Deputy Controller of the Western Downs Special Emergency Services, the SES.

Local SES volunteers from Miles, Chinchilla, Dalby and Tara went to the site of the shootings, and assembled there to hear in an organised, disciplined way how they could best help. It was SES members who manned the roadblocks, freeing up the thin blue line intent on rescue and containment. They bought with them as a matter of course mobile lighting and generators. They stayed on station, available, from the evening of the 12th to mid-morning 13th. Their presence and contribution were not noted by media until Harry Clarke of the *Country Caller* wrote 10 months later.

* * *

The shooters' next-door neighbours, retired couple Alan and Kerry Dare, heard the shooting. This was fairly normal in the area, though this time there was rather a lot of it. As Kerry put it, the gunshots 'just went on forever'. 'The explosions' – perhaps the petrol tank in the police car the Trains torched – and the rising black smoke galvanised them into action. Wildfire in grassland or bush is, after all, in no-one's good interest, and Al was a Rural Fire Brigade volunteer. Kerry said they suspected it was a house fire or a burning car.

The Dares did not know their neighbours' names. They 'waved to them several times' on walks that they often took on cool evenings. The neighbours had waved back.

Alan and a visiting friend, Vic Lewis, 70, did not linger once the smoke was obvious. They jumped into the nearest car, Vic's, and drove over to 251 in a hurry to see what they could do. Alan said on leaving Kerry, 'I'll be back.' Kerry got on the phone and got through to 000. The 000 operator, aware of the danger of shooters, talked of an 'incident… a job on'. He or she asked Kerry to stop Alan and Vic going there. Kerry rushed out. But it was too late: the men had left.

About 5pm their vehicle pulled up at the boundary gate to 251. Alan, the passenger, got out, maybe after ringing 000. He was using his phone to video the scene when he took a bullet in the back. He handed the phone to Vic, and fell to the ground.

Vic drove out, back to the Dare property. He was physically unharmed but agitated, confused and all over the shop emotionally. He handed over Alan's phone to Kerry, said Alan was 'in a bad way' and left. He knew no more than that then. No use trying to phone her man obviously, Kerry made her way out to Wains Road and headed to their neighbour's gate. How far she got is unknown.

Night fell, cloud came in and with it, the threat of stormy weather. Kerry kept trying to see her husband, but fearsome big men in body armour and balaclavas, with weapons across their chests, men who did not want to chat, turned her away, told her to leave, at a roadblock on Wains Road.

It was 6 am, nearly 13 hours after she had left her home, when she learned what happened to Alan. She felt that the police thought Alan was 'just a blockie' and her concerns and need to know were being ignored. Police officers in a situation like this are 100 precent focussed on eliminating threat to life and limb, temporarily absolved from the duties of community policing and good manners. But these Queensland ones reverted to being human beings when the threat was fixed and the facts came in.

In that early morning on Wains Road police officers formed an impromptu guard of honour as Alan Dare's body was driven away. It had become obvious that Al the blockie was a good neighbour, the sort of bloke most people would want living next door.

2
Training

Thou shalt not kill.
– Exodus 20:13 and Deuteronomy 5:17
King James Version Bible

Guardian Australia reporters Ben Smee and Nino Bucci looked at the nursery of the Train brothers. Their report into the men's father started thus: 'People who knew Ronald Train during his days living in Toowoomba joked that "no church would accept him, so he had to make his own".'[1]

I was reminded of some dating advice for women that I read somewhere long ago, source long forgotten. The column suggested women should be wary of men who had found enlightenment in obscure spiritual organisations, and, if the man under consideration founded or led a sect, 'run for the woods. For you, bears and wolves are trivial problems.' US preacher and cult leader Jim Jones had organised the ritual suicide (and the murder of those unwilling to drink the poisoned Kool-Aid) of over 900 of his adherents in 1978. Jim Jones: handsome, well-turned out sartorially, connections from NY to LA, an electric preacher/orator, with access to money, charismatic, a natural media performer, promiser of promises, promises, promises… including eternal life.

The wry observation about inventing his own church refers to his foundation, the Christian Independent Fellowship of Toowoomba (CIFT).

The constitution of CIFT includes a statement of faith that outlines Pastor Train's views on marriage:

We believe marriage between a man and woman is for life. We accept the scriptural teaching that God permits divorce, yet hates it. Remarriage, then, is never an option for either party whilst one or the other is still living.

* * *

Ronald Archie Train was born in Merriwa in the upper Hunter region of NSW in 1947. In his very early twenties, he married Gwyneth (Gwen) Mobberley. Four children were born of that union, Andrew, Gareth Daniel, Nathaniel Charles, and Namoi. Gwen died about three years before the Wieambilla killings. In December 2022 there was only dad, a great-grandfather.

The first-born child Andrew, and the last-born Naomi need not delay us long here. But two of his boys became cold-bloodied killers, so we look for links. The hideousness at Wieambilla cannot be sheeted home to their upbringing, though there are echoes.

Nathaniel Charles Train identified as Aboriginal, as did his sister. So does his son. A missing person notice described him 'as being of Aboriginal/Torres Strait Islander appearance'. Genealogical research on his paternal line leads back to a woman known only as Matilda but with blood connections to better known Aboriginals. Matilda was a domestic worker on the property of Len Cheetham, an early squatter around Gilgandra NSW, north of Dubbo. They had an illegitimate daughter in the 1890s. Records are old, scanty and patchy, too patchy to construct bloodline trees, but the researchers conclude that Nathaniel had every reason to believe Matilda was his '3 x great-grandmother' through the Cheetham-Cowley families though proof is absent.

In 2010 Naomi Train, shored up with a Diploma of Early Childhood and Care and teaching experience, had a decision to make. Would she take up a position with the Mobile Children's Service in Brewarrina or another classroom one on the north coast of NSW? She hit the road on what turned out to be a personal odyssey. At Brewarrina, 130 km west of Walgett, a sense of peace which she recognised from daily walks with her mum and dad, and her Christian faith, came over her. 'I didn't know about six months into it where I was... that I'd come home to Country,' Wailwan Country she discovered. She had also found what the Indigenous Australians would call her sitdown country . She took the Brewarrina job and her commute covers 1000 km 'in different directions through all kinds of terrain and [goes] to remote communities as well as properties in between' mentoring, teaching and talking with teachers, mums, dads, uncles, aunties, carers, elders, children and others, and dealing with the 'suits' in the education department electronically.

'We lost our heritage as a family. My Uncle found it. Myself and my Dad and my Uncle are really proud of who we are. It is not accepted in our family. My brother is starting to embrace who we are as a people.' Of Naomi's three brothers, Nathaniel, once of relatively nearby Walgett, is a strong possibility, but we cannot know.[3]

Pastor Ronald Archie Train trained at Malyon College in Brisbane which was established in 1904 as the Queensland Baptist College, and holds a master's degree in ministry from there. His special interests were 'theology and doctrine from New Testament documents', and he has been a prolific and arguably prolix writer of books on topics arising.

In 2013 he self-published *Without Absolutes, God is not God*. In 2014, *Protestant Shame*. And then, in 2016, *The Bridge to Eternal Life*.

Without Absolutes, God is Not God addresses issues 'such as God's self-revelation, the trinity, revelatory faith, and effective discipleship'. Ron, the Biblical scholar, presents two ways of thinking about, particularly, the New Testament: one, it is the Word of God; and two, it is the Word of God conveyed by humans. Pastor Ron is pro-absolutes. He says in the book:

> As a Christian it is foundational, I believe, to hold to absolutes. For example; a Christian should have absolutes about God's… being, absolutes about theology…, absolutes about Christology… and absolutes about… the Holy Spirit. Each of the foregoing absolutes, I believe, impact upon how one constructs a world view… why I have titled this collection of essays Without absolutes, God is not God… I guess the reader will be asking him or herself why is there a requirement to hold to absolutes. The need for absolutes is not complex. In reality the argument determines whether one is a believer or non-believer in the triune God. A believer will weigh whether God revelationally speaks into this world generally and specifically. A non-believer will object to such a proposition and as a consequence leave him or herself open to other belief systems. To perhaps put it another way a non-believer is faced with the choice of deciding whether God is a reality or whether God is a creation of human imagination…

He quotes much Scripture, confident his readers will know or look up 1 Corinthians 12:9 or Ephesians 2:8-9. He also quotes Revelatory Faith Evangelicals, existentialists, Martin Luther and Modernists. Faith stems from God; one cannot find faith by 'trial and argument', yet he seems to want to argue his readers into it.

The next year's *Protestant Shame* book has a villain: the freemasons. I know little about freemasonry, but in pre-Fitzgerald Queensland the state police commissioner's seat was alternately occupied by a 'kneeler' (Catholic, as at mass, the St Christopher Guild), then a 'gripper' (Protestant Masonic Lodge, after the coded secret handshake). This balancing of bigotries was an old Labor Party tradition continued under County Party rule.[4] This was true of the culture when Ron Train was growing up, but it has not been the case for 35 years. To finger freemasonry as a clear and present danger, or even a big deal, in the 2010s is a weird conspiracy theory.

I am convinced from my research and personal contact and confrontation with Freemasons that the sect of Freemasonry is a cancer within the Christian church and should never be tolerated...

Freemasons... do not in fact worship God but instead give their allegiance to Lucifer and accordingly worship this evil angel of light.

Pretty passionate stuff.

His last book has the audacious title *The Bridge to Eternal Life*. From his Introduction:

> Given that there are numerous books written about life after death, why write this book? The answer is that during my time in the Christian ministry I have observed, whilst providing pastoral care to people, that some have no certainty about eternal life; this is particularly so at funerals.

Now, who would have thought that?

> Hence, this book is being written in an Australian context to provide details of *eternal life*. Such a book, I believe, will provide assurance to the reader, assurance to one's faith and consolidation of one's world view.

Absolutism. The exposure of secret demons. Eternal life. Marriage for life.

The murderous sons were long (and absolutely) cut off from contact with their father long before he took up his pen or his sons their last guns. The preacher dedicates his books to his children, their partners, his grandchildren and great-grandchildren. As we will see, echoes survived.

* * *

Ronald Train first learned his sons and daughter-in-law were dead murderers on the morning of the day after the shootings, when police came to his door requesting a swab for DNA analysis and rock-solid biological identification. He spent the day, understandably, in 'delayed shock' and had a 'complete meltdown' that night. Nevertheless, the next day, 14 December 2022, he appeared exclusively on *A Current Affair*, in a seven-minute interview with Chris Allen.

The trolls got busy. They blamed him for not bringing his boys up properly. His grief – two sons dead – was ignored. His freely expressed sympathy for the victims of his sons' actions and their families was ignored. His, admittedly clumsily expressed, point that his sons were adults beyond his ken and control was ignored. A rumour that *A Current Affair* had paid him money for the interview was abroad and many poured out their outrage at this, forcing Channel Nine to issue a press release to the effect of not-a-cent-paid.

In the segment, Pastor Train seemed motivated by a duty to appear, though physically exhausted and emotionally drained. He was frank in reply to questions about his late sons' lives and the parental relationship. His sadness pervaded in everything he said. His recapped that he had talked with the police, and he was not talking again to media, 'I have lost two children' his last word. He has not answered media requests since.

* * *

Ronald Train's eldest child, son Gareth born 1975, and son Nathaniel, born the next year, had not had contact with him (or the late Gwen) 'for 23 years', not since 1999.

Schoolboy Gareth, dad said, had been a difficult child, emotionally 'volatile'. In his Brisbane and later Toowoomba schools he was 'very controlling' of others. Gareth was 'obsessed' with guns. Ammunition littered his bedrooms. He encouraged visitors to load or handle his rifles. Guns were sexy for Gareth; Nathaniel too, but much less so. (Unnamed others in other media reports harking back to those years, called Gareth 'a hot head' and Nathaniel 'cool-headed'; their father agrees.) The boys shot kangaroos, hares and rabbits for fun and entertainment, and for feral animal control. A lot of country boys do. I did. No big deal. Killing feral animals is, in the country, as much a duty as a sport. But an obsession with guns is a different matter.

Nathaniel did well in the classroom and on the tennis court. Gareth did not give a damn about academic matters, and in the Brisbane and the Toowoomba schools Gareth attended he was often in trouble, his father said.

Pastor Train conducted the marriage ceremony of son Nathaniel to Stacey Jane Christoffel in 1995 in the Baptist Church in Toowoomba. They had met and got to know each other in Ron's congregation in their teens; indeed, they were not out of their teens when they married.

When Nathaniel became a missing person, Ron Train, alerted by police inquiries, posted two messages on his Facebook page:

> Nathaniel is my youngest son. While we have not seen each other for 23 years, he is much loved.
>
> We trust our Lord is watching over his well-being.

Ron Train was seemingly not aware that Nathaniel and Stacey had divorced until after the Wieambilla killings. 'Gwen and I took a trip back in 2004 to Charters Towers to track them down, to try to talk to them, but they refused to let us into the house,' he reported to Chris Allen.

That is a lot of pain and suffering in one family.

1 'God and guns: the strict religious upbringing of the Wieambilla shooters', 15 December 2022

2 'Proud Aboriginal Man or Christian Terrorist?' *Dark Emu Exposed*, 28 February 2023

3 Rachael Knowles, 'Travelling teacher delivers education across remote communities', *National Indigenous Times*, 14 May 2020

4 Evan Whitton, *The Hillbilly Dictator: Australia's police state*, 1989; personal communication from Roger Rogerson

3

Nathaniel Train's Wanderings

Verily, verily, I say unto you, Hereafter ye shall see heaven open, and the angels of God ascending and descending upon the Son of man.

– Jesus to Nathaniel, John 1:51 King James Version Bible

Nathaniel Train was born in 1979 in Toowoomba, Queensland. He spent his boyhood there, and he met a girl there, Stacey Mary Christoffel. He was a Christian, part of the congregation of his father Pastor Ron Train's breakaway Baptist church (see Chapter 2).

Of young Stacey, little is known except that she left the congregation of her family's church to join Pastor Ron Train's church as a teenager. I doubt Stacey was into theology back then – though in her forties she would kill and die for a religious point of view, say Queensland's top cops and ASIO. Everything suggests that Nathaniel, a handsome youth, square jawed, with easy good manners, easy to talk to, maybe her first crush... was why she changed congregations. She set her cap on him and went for it. I suspect he was delighted.

They married in September 1995, in her 18th year, an important limit for brides and grooms in Queensland then. Under-18s faced problems and were required to show documentation like birth certificates, notes from a parent or guardian, an order from the federal Family Law Court or the Queensland Magistrates Court.

The couple had a daughter in 1996: Madelyn, who often uses 'Maddy' socially. Since the hideousness of December 2022, Madelyn has been the sole source of information to the media about her family's households and lifestyle.

Then a son, Aidan. In 2016 Aidan received an award at a ceremony for the 'highest achievement by an Aboriginal or Torres Strait Islander student in Queensland [in 2015]… Outstanding work… throughout [his] school career'. Out of this accolade, we learned that Aidan lived near his school, Spinifex State College, Mt Isa in the state's north-west while his parents worked elsewhere in Queensland. He won a Queensland Aboriginal and Torres Strait Islander Foundation scholarship. He culturally identified as 'a Wailwan man'. The Wailwan people's country is in central west New South Wales, around Warren. He excelled in maths and science and pursued tertiary studies. Since the tragedy of 2022, he has not spoken publicly.

The Train family purchased a $89,000 house in early 1997, in Cambooya, a small town 20 kilometres south of Toowoomba. On the title deed parents Ron and Gwyneth, Gareth, Nathaniel, Stacey and other family members were named as owners.

Within no more than two years after that, Gareth, Nathaniel and Stacey severed all association with Ron and Gwyneth. The parents' attempts to meet with or talk with them were rebuffed in no uncertain terms, and the estrangement continued after Gwyneth's death, and until the trio's own. It is not known why, but the timing and Ron's clear marriage-is-for-life belief suggests one: the two sons did not want their parents to know about the parting and unusual new pairing.

Around 1998-9, the marriage of Nathaniel and Stacey broke up, and they divorced. Madelyn, then three years old, said the split was an amicable one. Stacey thenceforth took up with and formed a family-of-four household with Nathaniel's older brother, Gareth. She may have legally married Gareth but if so, no-one has pinned the place or date. Nathaniel as a father figure became somewhat second-fiddle to Stacey's second husband in the lives of the children thenceforth.

Here, we backtrack and consider Nathaniel's work and wanderings.

* * *

At some stage Nathaniel must have gone through some sort of teacher training, as he was registered as a *bona fide* teacher by the then Queensland Board of Teacher Registration. There is no record of him having attaining a bachelor's degree. The Queensland Department of Education 'is committed to balancing personal privacy and the right to access information held by the department' which effectively means backtracking in the media's accounts of these years is dependent on the memories of those they could find, and published copy is contradictory. Stacey too must have undergone teacher training but when and where is another mystery.

In 1999 Nathaniel moved to Townsville. His first known teaching gig was at Bluewater State Primary School there.

In the early 2000s he worked as principal at Trinity Beach State School, in the suburban north of Cairns. Former student Reegan Hanley had only positive memories. "He was a great principal. You could walk down the hall and he'd be walking down opposite and he'd stop and have a conversation with you.'

In August 2004 the house in Cambooya was sold. Someone among 'the estranged family members' stumped up $15,000 to buy out Gareth and Stacey's shares. Although Nathaniel's name was on the original title, he was not listed as a vendor in the re-sale. Who lived in the house for the nine years before, or after the buyout is not known.

Nathaniel in 2004 was giving his address as 54 Barnard Drive,

Mt Sheridan in South Cairns. Gareth and Stacey gave the same address then too. Madelyn's memories of her biological parents and foster dad suggest this would not have been an unusual household set-up. But the media sleuths who found they were 'registered' as living there followed it up, and 'neighbours don't recall them'.[1]

However, the month after the Cambooya buyout, the three of them bought 4 hectares of land with a four-bedroom house on it at 34 River Road, Millstream, 120 kilometres south of Cairns, and the neighbours there do remember them: 'nasty, aggressive, paranoid people', who, in the first harbinger on the record of what's to come, strung barbed wire and set up floodlights and cctv there. It cost $107,000. Jumping forward five years with the real estate thread, the three sold #34 for $235,000, all three giving a phoney address next door to the school where Stacey and Gareth worked.

Nathaniel must have done something right at Bluewater, as he was appointed principal of Bentley Park College in Cairns six years later. While baffled parents and ex-colleagues have, in the wake of the killings, generally praised the mild-mannered man and the fine teacher who they thought they knew, two ex-pupils of Bentley Park remembered 2006 and Mr Train badly, and confidently predicted they could name a dozen more ex-pupils, especially indigenous ones, who shared their feelings. One, Chantel Kari, recalled being twice suspended without cause, and alleged enduring his racism. She described her grandmother's paper war with the Board of Education to keep her in the school. When Nathaniel left at the end of the year – Kari felt he was 'moved on' – she began to enjoy school again.[2]

His next gig was as the principal of Dimbulah State, Prep to Year 10, 150 students, 14 fulltime staff and others as aides. Dimbulah is on the Atherton Tablelands, over 100 kilometres west of Cairns. The town itself has a tad over 1000 inhabitants, but a lot of locals live around but not in it. More of the people who reside there are Italo-Australians than of any other ethnicity and the Catholic church offers St Anthony's as the town's alternative for local kids' schooling.

* * *

Innisfail East State School, Prep to Year 6, was among Australia's 10 per cent most disadvantaged primary schools. Half of the students are Aboriginal Australians. Student attitudes were such that it was not unusual for the students to refuse to take their feet off the desk when told to. Attendance was low. Academic results were lousy.

As the 'mild-mannered' principal of Innisfail East State, he instituted rigorous daily schedules for teachers and each class started with a chant by students calculated to make them memorise what they had learned. Teachers were encouraged not to waste a moment of class time on trivia, school business and the like. The accent was always on literacy and numeracy. Nathaniel spent the equivalent of two days teaching classes. There were regular, rigorous statistical analyses of results.

The school's results improved. Two years later the Grattan Institute analysed NAPLAN – National Assessment Program Literacy and Numeracy – that all Australians in Years 3, 5, 7 and 9 undergo – results for *The Australian* newspaper. Innisfail East scored above the national average in reading, writing and numeracy. 'I'm astounded at how quickly things have turned round,' he told *The Australian* in 2013.[3]

By 2017 he was at Yorkeys Knob State in a beach suburb of north Cairns; beach and suburb share the school's name. It had 250 students, around 30 to 40 of them Australian Aboriginals or Torres Strait Islanders, Prep to Year 6, and 19 fulltime teachers. He probably lived in an Ed department house at Keerawa Beach. Nathaniel was rising in his profession, doing well and learning how things work.

A mother of a schoolkid interviewed by the Channel Nine's *A Current Affair* team after the events at Wieambilla, remembered Nathaniel as 'a happy man' who 'loved kids, and kids loved him'. (She added that Nathaniel had had a 'bike accident' many years before and wore 'a prosthetic leg'. This is the sole reference to such a major life event, to radical last-choice surgery, and one usually with highly visible consequence. Yet no-one else has noted so much as a slight limp.) Whatever, he charmed that mother. She trusted him. So did Carla H, another mother of students there. 'He was always thinking about the kid's learning and futures. It's sad to see this has happened.' And Courtney P recalled how she and her husband chose to enrol their son at Yorkey's Knob State School because of Principal Train's reputation. 'I liked Mr Train. I liked his sound teaching ethos of bringing up children to be independent and responsible even at a young age.'

We know from his daughter Madelyn that Nathaniel worked very hard in these years, burning the midnight oil, skimping on sleep, eating irregularly and poorly, drinking too much coffee.

Yorkey's Knob State Year 3 clocked in among the top 20 Queensland NAPLAN achievement in 2018 on the Better Education rankings. In 2019 the school was # 25 in a ranking of Queensland's best NAPLAN results, and best primary school results in the Far North.[4]

He made the *Cairns Post* that year. If, as insiders say, all politics is local, then a local school principal's politics most certainly are, enrolments especially. The now much-reproduced photo of the happy head of school enjoying 'the kids' plaiting, painting and otherwise decorating his beard, a feature no child has, with Christmas-tree baubles, is a lovely one. His 'From the Principal' words in annual reports are steady, unremarkable ones.

After the killings, one parent said, 'I just don't get it. Mr Train was such a great person around the students. He helped my daughter transition into the school mid-year and without him playing tag with her every break, she wouldn't have done as well. When he was leaving, we went up to him and thanked him and his eyes welled up. Whatever has happened, we will always remember his good side. We are shocked.' Another recalled, 'He was quiet... he seemed stern but caring with the kids.' An ex-colleague said, 'He made Yorkeys the highest performing NAPLAN school in far north Queensland.'[5]

Nathaniel voluntarily resigned from Yorkey's in March 2020.

* * *

In 2020 Nathaniel worked as principal at Busy School Cairns – his photo remains on their website for now. This is one of now four such non-fee-paying Year 11 and 12 Busy schools in Queensland run by The Busy Group, a not-for-profit employment, training and support organisation. It is open to 16- to 19-year-olds who have done Year 10, 'and wish to re-engage with school, maybe get a Queensland Certificate of Education or go into tertiary education or apprenticeships'. Classes may be done while in paid employment or while engaged in other training. One-on-one teaching is emphasised. Besides being a second chance for teenagers who became disengaged with school, students who are parents or have a disability are accepted. In a media interview, Nathaniel said some of the school's enrolment came from the juvenile justice system. 'We don't take students that are highly violent or will endanger other students; we are a hand up not a handout.' Flexible as a rubber band, not like Yorkey's Knob State. Nathaniel did not stay long.

* * *

In that same year he became executive principal at Walgett Community College Primary School, in north-west New South Wales.

Walgett is where the Barwon and Namoi rivers meet. It once was a paddle-steamer port. It is a wool-, wheat-, hay- and cotton-growing area with opals as a sideline, as Lightning Ridge is, by western NSW standards, close by. The town has more than 2000 souls residing there, the local government area hosts more than 6000. Of them, somewhere between 43 and 70 percent are descendants of the First Australians who lived there before 1788, most of them of the Gamilarary, Yuwoalarary and Ngayimba mobs.

Walgett is a town of shuttered shopfronts and two hotels, the Gateway and the Oasis. The suicide rate, particularly youth suicides, is high. Domestic violence and sexual assault rates are high. Drug use, especially or perhaps most problematically, alcohol and methamphetamine, too is high.

Since 2003, when pre-school, primary and secondary education were put under one roof, the town has had one state school, the modern well-equipped Walgett Community College, for around 150 students, 14 percent of them Aboriginal Australian students. Few schools have been the subject of as much adverse publicity and controversy as the WCC. Teachers have been assaulted, one struggling out of what seems to have been an attempt to garrotte her. Another, pregnant at the time, felt she had to physically intervene in a brawl among students wherein a knife was seen to have been produced. Police have been called there quite regularly: at one stage a police station on-campus was proposed, but the proposal was quashed by, among others, the influence of Aboriginal elders with whom the WCC worked closely under the Connected Communities policy. The school's log book recorded 50 violent incidents in one two-year period; hardly a fortnight passing without one. The WCC instituted a 'lockdown' response procedure more reminiscent of prisons than schools – classroom blinds are pulled down, doors locked, silence to prevail until word was received that the threat had passed. In 2021, Executive Principal N Train's second year there, only 10 of the 21 teacher positions were filled. Principals do not stay long either: 20 in 15 years. As the executive principal in primary Years, he was spared dealing with most of the more troublesome older students.

Nathaniel Train had the support of the elders. One who, like other residents, did not want to be named, described him as 'wonderful. He was making some really important changes. We were supportive of him and trusted his intelligence.' Many of the teachers liked him and some community members were also supportive.[6]

But other people in the town did not like him, and felt he was too strict. 'He wouldn't even let parents into the front gate of the school,' one teacher or parent recalled. Some in the Indigenous community described him as racist, though Nathaniel's claim to have Aboriginal blood in his veins, culture in his head, was well known.

He met and married Vanessa De Jager. They either moved to Walgett together or she was a colleague at the school. They were a familiar sight, walking their dog around town. They planned to build a home at Moruya on the NSW South Coast and an architect was working on it. They spent Christmas in a caravan on site.

In August 2021, in the middle of Term 3, Nathaniel was at his office desk at the school when he suffered a sudden, unexpected, massive heart attack.

An assistant principal and a school counsellor performed CPR, and worked on keeping him breathing and pumping blood. Paramedics got him to hospital. The 42-year-old was granted departmental medical leave. This may have lengthened his time on their books, as Covid-19 vaccination became compulsory for NSW teachers working in schools in November that year, and Nathaniel Train was firmly anti-vaxx.

One of the cardiac event's legacy was impaired mental health. When deprived of oxygen too for long, the brain's frontal lobes – the seat of personality, reasoning, emotions and judgement – are damaged. Survivors experience memory loss, have difficulty in paying attention and concentrating, and become more impulsive; paranoia, suspiciousness and an inability to plan or cope with pressure are common. These symptoms may disappear in time, but for some they are permanent. There is no clinical evidence this happened with Train – Queensland Police will no doubt investigate his health records, medications prescribed and provide an autopsy report for the coroner – but colleagues and associates in Walgett noted personality 'changes' and 'anger' in him.[7]

When anybody asked Vanessa how Nathaniel was doing since the heart attack, she would walk away. She took over liaison in the building work at Moruya.

Madelyn reported he hated taking heart medication but felt forced to.[8]

By March of the following year the NSW Department of Education and Nathaniel Train wound up employer-employee matters, his letter of resignation accepted; or sacked after seven months absence from duties. The Department is silent on which. Nathaniel was off their books.

But not out of their hair. He had, he believed, evidence of cheating in annual NAPLAN tests. The issue seems to have begun at Walgett when a student who shared a surname with a teaching aide got the answers to Questions 1 and 2 wrong, and Questions 3 to 36 inclusive right.

In March 2022 he bombarded the Department with emails, 16 over a two-week period to one secretary. One recipient said of the emails, 'They were quite out there. His mental health deteriorated post-Walgett.' He felt ignored, and probably was. He took the issue to the Ombudsman; the Hon Roy Butler, Member of the NSW Parliament; the Hon Senator for Queensland Pauline Hanson; and the Hon Mark Latham, Member of the NSW Legislative Council. Latham, chair of the upper house education committee, said Nathaniel Train 'wasn't ranty' to him, 'but he was certainly bitterly disappointed with the education department'. Latham raised the cheating question in Macquarie Street at a budget estimates committee in May 2022. His last contact with Train was in July that year. What he said about Walgett Community College did not go down well with its teachers. When he visited Walgett in 2020, they held a sign:

MARK LATHAM NOT WELCOME ON FIRST NATIONS LAND

* * *

We now know more about what Nathaniel Train did after his sick leave ended.

He drove north in a black Toyota LandCruiser 200 Series with bull bars, a vehicle registered in NSW, into Queensland. It was eight sleeps before Christmas 2021 the day he hit the border. It had only a few days before been opened, but opened only to coronavirus-vaccinated travellers. The Boongangar Bridge over the McIntyre River was an unmanned border post requiring the swipe of an e-pass to open. Someone had tried to ram open the gate on the bridge without success. Then someone had taken an angle-grinder to the lock. Nathaniel would become the prime suspect for these acts. It had a camera recording the plates of vehicles that crossed.

The McIntyre River runs into the Weir River which runs into the Barwon River, and it forms part of the state line between NSW and Queensland. Floodwaters are frequent there. Goondiwindi on the McIntyre is protected by 11-metre-high levees and has seen floodwater rise to over 10.5 metres. Although Nathaniel had got over the bridge, the McIntyre was in flood and not finished with him. He successfully drove through one branch of the flooded river but in the next one, water drowned his engine. A farmer from Goondiwindi, Queensland side, found Nathaniel in camo gear on the flooded road and watched him 'dumping all the stuff out of the car and throwing it into the creek'. The farmer arranged to tow the LandCruiser to his place as it was blocking the roadway. While farm workers pulled the LandCruiser out, the farmer talked to the traveller, who said he was Nathaniel Train, principal of the Walgett Community College. By way of explanation for being there – it is not the most well-travelled or easiest route – he said he was an anti-vaxxer prevented from travelling to see his family in Queensland.

When the vehicle was at his place drying out, the farmer turned to seeing the traveller on his way. A local offered to drive the wheelless motorist to Talwood in his own driveable vehicle. Nathaniel accepted and got two firearms, both registered to him it turned out, a bow, arrows and 'military "Rambo" knives' from the LandCruiser and put them in the local's vehicle.

The local also lent Train a phone to make a call. When Nathaniel was on the line, he spoke, said the local, 'in a code which involved a Morse code-type scenario saying "dot dot, dash dash".'

He dropped Train off near Talwood, where he understood the man had arranged to be picked up.

Days later, the water level dropped and a Fijian farm worker said, 'Hey, look at all this stuff next to the fence!' Besides a lot of paperwork from Walgett College, a shotgun, a camouflage-painted rifle with a telescopic sight and another rifle were found where the 4WD had been bogged. These were handed to police.

The 4WD, checked and found not to be on the stolen motor vehicles list, was abandoned. It sat a year in the farmer's paddock until events in Wieambilla a year later saw it taken to Goondiwindi Police Station. Vanessa wants it back at some stage.

In April 2022 a Goondiwindi police officer following up the illegal entry at the e-gate collected statements from the farmer and the local referred to above.[9]

Where Nathaniel went after Talwood and how he travelled is not yet known.

We know of course where he ended up: 251 Wains Road Wieambilla Queensland 4413.

* * *

After the point when Nathaniel and Vanessa had split up, they stayed in contact with each other until 9 October 2022. After that, her attempts to contact him failed; he did not call back or reply to texts or emails, and this abrupt change in behaviour, together with his post-cardiac mental condition, had her worried.

Nathaniel told daughter Madelyn he aimed to reconnect with God in nature. "That's why he was living that way,' camping on the Wieambilla property as she understood the situation. Maddy says the Trains repeatedly told her not to get involved. 'They asked to be left alone multiple times,' she said. 'They told Vanessa "Don't report him missing. He doesn't want to see you. Leave him alone".'[10]

On 4 December she reported how he had gone incommunicado to local NSW police.

On 8 December the police issued a public missing person report, widely disseminated on social media. It came to the attention of Gareth, who sent Vanessa what have been described as 'vicious, threatening messages', their actual contents not released. For Vanessa, not a squeak from her husband of no fixed address that she knew of.

Two days after that publication, Nathaniel came up to a horse rescuer David Maynard and said he knew of three horses that may need looking after. 'Do you have room?' he asked. Maynard, who had never met Train before, had a paddock or two out of Tara where he looked after about 20 horses. Sometimes he offers campers sites for their tents on it: 'Just bring carrots.' He thought Train was 'just a person struggling to pay for his horses'. Owning hayburners can be expensive. 'He was absolutely calm… He was peaceful.'[11]

And two days after that, his last, Nathaniel Train, 46, was holding a long arm with intent to kill unsuspecting, defenceless police he did not know.

1 Daily Mail Australia, 15 December 2022; updated 21 January 2023

2 Kylie Stevens, *Daily Mail Australia*, 14 December 2022

3 *Australian* no date

4 Bad Apple Bullies https://www.badapplebullies.com/

5 Kylie Stevens, Daily Mail Australia, 14 December 2022

6 Jordan Baker, *Sydney Morning Herald*, 13 December 2022

7 Jordan Baker, *Brisbane Times*, 14 December 2022

8 Kevin Airs, *Daily Mail Australia*, 30 January 2023

9 Rory Callinan, *ABC News*, Talwood, 20 December 2022

10 Kevin Airs, *Daily Mail Australia*, 30 January 2023

11 Candace Sutton, 'School principal and his brother… hail of bullets', *Daily Mail Australia*, 14 December 2022

4
In Search of Stacey Train

And Ruth said, Intreat me not to leave thee, or to return from following after thee: for whither thou goest, I will go; and where thou lodgest, I will lodge: thy people shall be my people, and thy God my God: Where thou diest, will I die, and there will I be buried: the Lord do so to me, and more also, if ought but death part thee and me.

– Ruth 1: 16-17 King James Version, Bible

Stacey Mary Jane Train was a daughter of the Christoffel family. Her 'sisters were understood to have been at their parents' home in North Queensland' when they all heard the news that Stacey was a dead murderer in her mid-forties.[1]

In the hours following that news, when calls from journalists to people named 'Christoffel' stacked up, they may have decided on family spokespersons to do an interview, after which they would stay silent, for nothing further has been heard from them since Joe Hinchliffe's item was published three days after the killings.

One of the two anonymous family members called Stacey 'a quiet girl who was always somehow the odd one out'.

The Christoffel children grew up in the congregation of one of the Baptist churches in the city of Toowoomba, a 100-minute drive west from

Brisbane. In her teens, Stacey left that congregation for Pastor Ronald Train's breakaway Christian Independent Fellowship of Toowoomba, CIFT. It may have been something in the pastor's fundamentalist, conservative theological brew that attracted her. Or it could have been a boy: the pastor's son Nathaniel. They were an item from high-school days and married in 1995 when she was 18. Family spokesperson: 'I wish she never did [join CIFT]. This [the shootings] would never have happened.'

The couple had two children. Nathaniel's older brother Gareth had at times joined their households. When the marriage ended after three to four years, Stacey re-married, Gareth.

The Christoffel family had no reason to like Gareth Train. Stacey's mother would call Stacey on Stacey's birthday each year, in the hope of a break in the barriers that had estranged them for a long time. Sometimes, mum got to leave a message. But if Gareth picked up, she would kill the call immediately. It was, in the family spokesperson's view, Gareth's 'controlling' behaviour that had created and upheld the severing of the Christoffel family's contact with her. 'I knew Gareth was an arsehole when he took over his brother's wife. It was all downhill from there. Now she is dead because of them.'

* * *

Stacey and Nathaniel's eldest, daughter Madelyn, went public after the shootings. If Madelyn's memory serves her well, the 'amicable divorce' of Stacey and Nathaniel occurred when she was three, about 1999, when Nathaniel was at Bluewater, his first teaching post.

She appeared on two exclusive Channel Nine News items and on Nine's *A Current Affair*. The Nine organisation's own Ray Hadley was furious and lambasted the organisation's news bosses on his Radio 2GB *Morning Show:* 'Stop it. They're murderers. The cops were executed.'

True, but thus he effectively shut down the only voice from within any of the wandering Trains' various tents and one who was in contact with them right up to their ends.[2] No-one became better informed about the murderers after this outburst; 9.99 percent of Australians' hearts, like Ray Hadley's and mine, were with the victims. For their heads, Madelyn had things to contribute.

It is universally presumed in media reports that Stacey and Gareth got legally married. But there is no when or where, and the moniker 'Mrs Train' is no help. Whatever, they seem to have been a family unit of four from the get-go, and, in Madelyn's recall, a happy and gentle one. Contact with Nathaniel was never a problem. If there was a gun nut around in her childhood years, it had to be Nathaniel not Gareth. (The men's father remembered that was very different in their boyhoods.) Madelyn recalled Stacey 'hated' guns.

Stacey must have completed some sort of teacher training in the early 2000s. In the early 2000s she and both the brothers often resided at the same address, so Nathaniel may have encouraged that.

The Queensland Department of Education's curious policy means Stacey's employment history below has been stitched together from media reports of the memories of ex-students, their parents, teaching colleagues and ex-neighbours. Memories over nearly quarter of a century can, and usually do, sometimes fail. There are holes in what is known.

In February 2004, Stacey began her teaching career at the Charters Towers State High School.

By 2007 Stacey was a head of department at Herberton State School. The school won an award for Indigenous education excellence.

In 2009 Stacey was principal at Proston State School, west of Gympie.

In 2010 she became a staff member at Quinalow State School in a western suburb of Toowoomba.

In 2011 Stacey attended a five-day Indigenous-led Stronger Smarter school leaders' training course at the Aboriginal community of Cherbourg.

That year she took up a teaching position at Camooweal State School. Camooweal, population 200, is as far west as you can get in northern Queensland; the area borders the Northern Territory, and falls within the local government area of Mt Isa, the basis of Mt Isa's claim to have the longest main street in the world, the Barkly Highway, 188 kilometres. Very dry, very hot in summer. A teaching vacancy there would not attract many applications.

Camooweal local Karen Sullivan, whose kids attended the school, met Stacey and Gareth: 'He was just crazy. He was a control freak. They didn't bring a good vibe to the community.' Another resident, a school support-staffer, recalled, in 2022, her first meetings with Stacey and Gareth. 'We were invited to tea to their house, to welcome them to the town. The first thing I noticed was they had their pig dogs inside the house in cages and Gareth had a big collection of hunting knives and he then told us he was a social worker.' (Gareth and his dogs we'll cover in Chapter 5.) While this is Stacey's story, Gareth's presence, dogs, attitude and behaviour swamped whatever Stacey did or aimed to do. An ex-pupil remembered Mrs Train instituting a program to stop bullying. This good-intentioned program, probably the fruits of the NSW Department of Education's Sydney policy wonks a long way from the chalkface in the state's Outback, was imposed on teachers. Whatever Stacey did, the program 'only seemed to encourage the bullies' in the view of the ex-pupil. 'If you complained you immediately got detention. I had lots of mates whose parents pulled them out of the school.' The school support-staffer said Gareth 'quickly took over the school' and 'ended up dominating the parents and friends committee'.

Outside school, the Trains did not socialise. Karen Sullivan: '[Gareth] was always there with her. He was a control freak. She could never say anything.'

There was too an ugly incident of domestic violence. A resident, Minnie Walsh, one with an attendance officer role in the school, once saw Gareth drag Stacey up a set of stairs by her hair: 'It's a high house and he was just dragging. I thought "it's none of my business" and I didn't like to interfere so I didn't say anything.'

Students left. And in 2012 or 2014 Stacey left Camooweal State too.

In 2015 she taught at Happy Valley State School. This Mt Isa primary school used to be called Isa Mine State School. Like most schools in Mt Isa Happy Valley is 'mineside' – not 'townside' – of the Leichhardt River. The big local issue of the day was that 10 percent of local children had dangerously high levels of lead in their blood. Where had the lead come from? Glencore's smelters or the local soils? Plenty of room for a conspiracy theory there, but no sign Stacey ran with that one.

She and Gareth purchased their Wieambilla block in February 2015 but would not move onto it for four years. The homestead was rented out at times.

After a year in Mt Isa Valley, Stacey and Gareth moved to the Far North, to Pormpuraaw State School, prep to Year 7, in 2016. Stacey was principal. Pormpuraaw is an Aboriginal community of around 750 people today, over 80 percent of them Aboriginal or Torres Strait Islanders, on the west coast of the Cape York Peninsula. The school, like much of the town's infrastructure, derives from an Anglican mission which had long before handed over control to the Queensland Department of Aboriginal and Island Affairs. Half the school's staff are Aboriginal Australians. The town is governed by the elected Pormpuraaw Aboriginal Shire Council drawn from the Thayore, Wik, Bakanh and Yir Yoront clans there. Like the school, the shire's logo depicts a crocodile. A commercial crocodile farm, exporting skins for handbags and so on, and a cattle station exist. Fishing and bird watching bring in a few tourist dollars. The cost of living was high: generator-only electricity, expensive petrol and, during The Wet, all milk, fruit and vegetables had to be flown in. Gareth too was employed at Pormpuraaw State, as groundsman. But the Council was said to have grown unhappy with the principal. They left.

On 24 June 2016, Stacey was appointed Acting Principal of Mitchell State School 'for a term'. Mitchell, population 1000 or so, and the school had around 130 Prep to Year 10 students. Year 11 and 12 students bus 90 km to Roma. The town is on the flood-prone Maranoa River, the Warrego Highway and the Western Railway, serving the cattle- and sheep-raising region. The school has a heritage-protected '1914 Building' on site.

Curiously, Mitchell's history includes the murder of a police officer. In March 1902 an arrest warrant was issued on the Kenniff brothers, Patrick and Jimmy, for stealing a pony. Patrick had form in NSW and Queensland for cattle and horse stealing and other crimes of dishonesty, and since the brothers' father took up a property there, cattle soon began to go missing and their owners soon got angry. Constable George Doyle, station manager Arthur Dahlke and blacktracker Sam Johnson located the brothers' bush camp, fell on it, and nabbed Jimmy and his 18 year-old brother, but Patrick escaped capture. Johnson walked back to where the pursuers had left their pack horses, to bring them up to the camp and continue in pursuit for Patrick. When he got back Doyle and Dahlke were gone but the Kenniffs were back, intent on overpowering him. He evaded them and advised the town.

A second, larger posse went out. They found evidence of a gun fight at the camp site. Then a horse associated with Doyle was located, saddle bags full of charcoal and some personal effects identified as being Doyle's or Dahlke's. The Kenniffs had burnt their bodies to hide evidence, and intended to scatter and hide the unburnt.

A £1,000 reward was issued. A police manhunt combed the area, and on 23 June the brothers were taken at what became known as Arrest

Creek, just south of Mitchell. A complicated legal case involving the Privy Council in London ensued. Jimmy escaped the rope but Patrick was hanged in Boggo Road Gaol. Today, the Kenniffs are considered two of the last of the bushrangers.

* * *

Stacey Train got a job as a head of curriculum and teacher or teachers' aide at Tara Shire State School in 2019. The title means that, aside from teaching classes, she was responsible for charting coverage of items that the department's program had stipulated be taught, were in fact covered – for example, that all Year 8s had been taught about photosynthesis or the geometry of solids or a Shakespearean play.

On the Western Downs now, they moved into 251 Wains Road.

But, in a curious note, multiple parents whose children attend Tara Shire State College could not remember Stacey Train.[3] She was said to be a branch delegate for the Queensland Teachers Union in 2019. What branch isn't known, but a Western Downs one looks likely.

In August 2021, she took several weeks' leave to tend to Nathaniel after his heart attack, presumably in NSW. By then the coronavirus, restrictions, vaccinations, opinions, prejudice and arguments were raging.

She quit that job, and resigned from the Queensland Department of Education, in December 2021. An anti-vaxxer, she quit the school the day before a no-jab/no-school-job rule came into force. She had arguments – moral, political and health arguments with a conspiratorial twist – but she had burned a bridge. She told colleagues she and Gareth had enough money to get by, but economic and social independence of Gareth was no longer an option. Psychological, intellectual and emotional independence likewise?

Tara residents agreed they had not seen Stacey in the township 'for at least a year' in December 2022.[4] John, a Wieambilla blockie, did meet her, however. They fell to talking about some Tara young people who had been 'acting out' at the time. Stacey said, 'They all need to be put in a hole and shot.' John thought that a bit extreme but just said, 'They just need a kick up the arse.'

* * *

From her early twenties, after she had experienced boarding school life and years of independent living, Madelyn Train clearly saw that Gary (as she called Gareth) was entertaining weirder and weirder conspiratorial theories as Covid-19 raged on and on.

Madelyn's contacts with her mother by phone, text and email were filled with an obsessiveness familiar to her: Gary's, not Stacey's. The pattern was similar too. Small talk and news would be quickly steered to crazy stuff. Madelyn figured it was the websites they visited generating algorithms that presented them with more of the same, as algorithms do, and that they were spending far too much time online.

At 6:34pm 12 December 2022 she got a text from Gareth: 'People have been sent to kill us.'

Mystified, a bit alarmed, entirely ignorant of the killings two hours before then and the siege that was underway, she texted him back, asking, among other questions, if her mother was all right.

Stacey made no reply. Nobody did.

* * *

My search for what led Stacey Train to decide to kill and die that day has ended in failure.

An anonymous source said Stacey was an active shooter, and when wounded by a police bullet, kept shooting until a bullet killed her.

Queensland Police have since revealed they have recovered diaries she penned and that these throw light on the trio's beliefs and motivations. The coroner will read and probably, hopefully publish these, but I suspect that these will be apocalyptic rubbish; that a clearer understanding of what made the woman tick will still elude us; and the diaries will simply hold up a mirror to the rantings of the strongest personality at 251 Wains Road: Gareth Train.

Stacey seems to have been one of nature's spear carriers, loyal to the ideas, rule, chosen path of whosoever would lead her, likely one of nature's dominant personalities. Recall the words of one of her family: Stacey was 'a quiet girl who was always somehow the odd one out'? Recall too the parents of the children she presumably taught at Tara State who couldn't remember any Stacey Train being there? Few ex-students have emerged either. There is no evidence of friendships enjoyed outside the home and, her daughter aside, no-one has come forward to say she had a virtue or a vice or was in any way worthy of note.

Yet she wholeheartedly threw herself into these monstrous, barbaric acts and I suspect she died smug in the righteousness of what she did.

---

1 https://www.qatsif.org.au/stories/2018/4/16/qatsif-student-aidan-train-named-as-2015s-highest-achiever

2 'Stop airing this stuff': Ray Hadley slams Nine for giving cop killers' daughter airtime, *Daily Telegraph*, 2 February 2023

3 *Daily Mail Australia*, 15 December 2022; updated 21 January 2023

4 Ditto

5
Gareth Train

Therefore I am full of the fury of the Lord*; I am weary with holding in: I will pour it out upon the children abroad, and upon the assembly of young men together: for even the husband with the wife shall be taken, the aged with him that is full of days.*
– Jeremiah 6:11 King James Version Bible

We left the earliest knowledge of young Gareth David Train that we have in his father's recollection (Chapter 2). Gareth, said his dad, was 'very difficult to control, very overpowering and I just think that in the end he took over that relationship that Nathaniel and Stacey had because Gareth and Nathaniel were fairly close, because they were the two brothers next to each other,' he told Channel Nine's Chris Allen for *A Current Affair* within 48 hours of learning that his long-estranged sons were dead killers. Young Gareth was obsessed with guns, ammunition all over his bedroom floor. A 'hot head' in contrast to his level-headed brother. Problem at schools in Brisbane and Toowoomba. On the 'Asperger's spectrum'.

I believe Gareth David Train's overriding will was the prime mover of the hideousness on 12 December 2022.

* * *

What was the source Gareth's will? Could Asperger's Syndrome be part of the answer? Investigators may uncover medical records of relevance, anti-psychotic medication records say, but in the meantime, Asperger's is the only diagnosis we have.

Asperger's is a medical and psychological term falling into disuse, as its symptoms are now said to be comfortably housed on the autism spectrum disorder, ASD, in places like the pages of the DSM-5, the hugely influential (and controversial) *Diagnostic and Statistical Manual of Mental Disorders* Edition 5, one of the biggest-selling academic books in the world.

What has not changed is that people with, say Asperger's, generally have no problems with learning, remembering, solving problems, paying attention and concentrating; and they can listen and talk OK. Some indeed are super bright, highly creative and succeed at things that require them as individuals to focus, persist, ignore distractions and undergo repetitive behaviour (like solo practice or rehearsals). This is why many think ASD helped Albert Einstein crack relativity and Satoshi Tajiri invent Pokémon. In business and the arts, the roll call is impressive: from Bill Gates, Steve Jobs and the founders of Getty Images, to Courtney Love, Daryl Hannah and Anthony Hopkins. Those who are diagnosed with ASD find it extreme difficulty to communicate with others. Humour and irony are lost on them, and metaphors confuse them. They commonly avoid eye contact and their faces can seem blank, deadpan and expressionless. Social interaction can often make them anxious, confused and frustrated. So, rigid behaviour patterns and social withdrawal are their favoured solutions. Their focus is intense on a particular topic. Everything else bores them. They lack empathy – the ability to see the world through the eyes of others.

About 35 per cent of 'auties', as many with ASD like to call themselves, may exhibit psychotic symptoms like hallucinations, voices only they can hear and hold delusional beliefs, beliefs that stem from a lack of understanding of expected social conventions.

Because some famous auties have led organisations, a link between ASD and leadership skills has been looked into. The jury is still out.

The vast majority of auties are law-abiding people. Some can be stubbornly pedantic about following the rules they have learned, waiting for a green 'walk' light to cross a road clearly empty of all traffic in both directions at 3 am for example. People with ASD are only marginally more likely to commit crimes than people in the general populations, and even then, the figures are rubbery. But diagnosis or post-mortem suspicions have highlighted famous criminals like serial killer Jeffery Dahmer, Sandy Hook school shooter Adam Lanza and Port Arthur shooter Martyn Bryant. Debate continues.

There we leave, for now, the only psychiatric or psychological clue to Gareth Train's bizarre behaviour and beliefs.

* * *

Soon after the marriage of Nathaniel and Stacey Christoffel, Gareth and Nathaniel in their early twenties ceased all contact with their parents and probably siblings – forever, as it turned out. The daughter of that marriage, Madelyn, has said she understood that the Train brothers spoke out about being sexually molested as children by an unnamed man known to the family. When the family did not believe them, the curtain came down. No charges were laid then, and the alleged paedophile had died before Madelyn Train spoke. The rift was absolute: the boys' father, unlike members of the Christoffel family, was unaware Gareth had married Stacey until news of the shooting revealed it was so.

About the time of Gareth's union with Stacey, he was charged with unlawful possession of a firearm. He had allowed his Queensland gun licence to expire. This rather minor blemish aside, his criminal record would remain clean until his death.

Gareth's early years with Stacey were spent following her from one Department of Education job to another, covered in Chapter 4. When they first set up together, Madelyn was three and Aidan younger. Gareth's main contribution seems to have been, and Madelyn has confirmed, domestic and child minding. Nathaniel often joined their household for short and long sojourns and the trio were often registered as living at Nathaniel's or at Gareth and Stacey's or at fictitious addresses.

In 2004 the three purchased a property and house, and the first reports of barbed wire, floodlights and cctv cameras emerge. In early 2009 they – all three registered as living at a fictitious address in Proston in the then-new local government area of South Burnett – sold the house, and started that year cashed up.

Gareth's later claim to be a 'social worker' and an authority on police corruption seems to rest on a job he got that year as a child safety support officer with the state Department of Communities' child safety and disability services in South Burnett. Unlike the tight-lipped education department, the current Department of Child Safety, Youth Justice and Multicultural Affairs cheerfully reported he lasted two months.[1] The circumstances of his leaving are not known. The area's head office is in Kingaroy, 225 km northwest of Brisbane, and Proston, where Stacey was a school principal, is a further 65 km northwest, a big commute even by rural Queensland standards. If he liaised with the station in Proston, population around 300, he would not have known many police officers, maybe two or three; if with Kingaroy, population over 7000, probably about the same number due to specialisation.

His next employment was a Department of Education groundsman at Stacey's school, Proston State, a job pattern discussed in Chapter 4. When she was teaching in Mt Isa's Happy Valley State in 2014, Gareth was employed for a time, presumably as groundsman or similar, across the river at Mt Isa Special State, a school for students with intellectual disabilities. When she was at Pormpuraaw State, Gareth worked at the school in an unknown capacity but there were complaints, and he quit that job.

But it was at Camooweal State 2010-11 where Gareth revealed himself as a bizarre and arrogant individual, a control freak and a cruel bastard.

* * *

In 2011 Stacey was appointed to the teaching staff of Camooweal State School, and brought Gareth along with her. Although son Aidan reported being bought up in and around remote Queensland schools, he was too old to attend this Prep-to-Year-6 one. So, just the two of them.

Camooweal is a scatter of old houses, a pub and mostly empty shops straddling the Barkly Highway about 13 km from the Northern Territory, with around 200 residents.

The presumably Department of Education house they occupied backed onto the school grounds. It is not clear how many staff the school employed then, but in the 2020s there were less than a dozen including teaching, non-teaching and indigenous staff.

Gareth was hired as the school's gardener, cleaner and groundsman. He also wrangled the position of secretary of the Parents and Friends Committee. At parent-teacher meetings he would sit in on them or occupy a seat just outside the door. His domineering attitude was noted. He did a lot to make himself offensive and resented, and he succeeded.

Gareth's two-year sojourn in Camooweal was mainly remembered for what he did with the pig dogs he ran. As we've seen, he kept them in cages inside their house. While the Australian Pig Doggers & Hunting Association's Code of Ethics has rules about kennels (access to fresh water at all times, must be kept clean, hygienic and odour-free, etc), keeping pig dogs inside with humans did not seem to have even occurred to them. Dogging involves the dog scenting, running down and holding the feral pig by the ears until the hunter arrives and kills the pig with a knife thrust to the heart, or a shot in the head or the heart. Doggers need a large 'sticking knife' to kill the beast and/or to bleed out the carcass, and another, perhaps two, to skin it. Gareth reportedly had 'a big collection' of knives. Knives for knives' sake?

Gareth took his dogs to the local swimming hole. One child of that time recalled, 'We would often find the gutted carcases of pigs there. Sometimes we would see Gareth with his knives running around with the dogs chasing the pigs. We would hear the boars screaming as he gutted them.' This is the collective memory of country kids, kids used to the slaughter of farm animals for the larder or dog tucker. When they say Gareth took the guts out of conscious animals, they would know exactly what an unnecessary, inhumane departure from the norm they are talking about. The motivation to put on show like this for children is chilling. Criminal psychologists have long noted cruelty to animals is a trait common in the childhoods of psychopaths, serial killers, and the like, but these are the actions of an adult man, seemingly to impress or inspire fear in children.

Sometimes, Gareth would bring whole carcasses home and hang them up by their hind trotters for butchering. Another ex-pupil: 'Then he would butcher them and the blood and offal would be running directly out of their yard onto the school oval. There would be a smell of offal and blood running onto the footy field.' Complaints were made. Nothing was done.

The APDHA code recommends removing the offal at the kill site and slicing open the stomach to aid the speed of decomposition. Gareth did not lighten his load – an un-gutted feral boar averages 80 to 100 kilograms – in this easy-to-do, usual way. It is hard to avoid the view

Gareth was putting on a show: that he would do whatever he wished, wherever he wished, whenever he wished, and nobody could stop him.

The APDHA code also insists pig dogs be registered with the local council (and so collared) and vaccinated by a veterinarian. It is not known if Gareth complied or not, but his attitude to government and vaccination was later hostile. The code has a no-dumping-in-public-places rule regarding carcasses he clearly did not give a damn about.

He and his dogs became locally notorious. It was remembered he sat in his yard watching them mate. He let his dogs out to attack other dogs.

His driving too earned note. It was implied he drove past those walking on the side of the road in a deliberately intimidating manner. One parent recalled, 'He would come over the grid at 100 kilometres and he would miss me by an inch.'

His dominating 'control-freak' attitude to his cowered wife and an episode of physical coercion of her was recalled in 2022. Outside of the school, the Trains never socialised. In and around school, Gareth dominated.

Gareth took a lot of liberties for a groundsman. One mother reported, 'If he heard [students] swearing, he would send them home. He would put their arms up behind their backs in an arm lock and march them home. I caught him doing it one day and told him, "If you touch my son like that you will be in trouble." We ended up with no kids at the school.'

Numerous complaints were made to Education Department officers at Mt Isa and Brisbane, to local politicians and even to a local priest, perhaps because of Stacey's Christian beliefs. There is a mystery concerning his interaction with local police.

Many students left Camooweal State. And in 2011 Stacey and Gareth left too.

* * *

The Pormpuraaw Aboriginal Shire Council, community and local families became increasingly unhappy with the Trains over the course of 2016, according to a community worker. Early that year Gareth had resigned from the Education Department. They left amid complaints.

Although his stepdaughter recalled him applying, Gareth, in his early forties at thatpoint, did not appear to have worked at a job again.

* * *

After the buyout of the two brothers and Stacey in the Train clan's Cambooya property in August 2004, the trio in the next month purchased the property previously mentioned that they lived in for a time and fortified. This property was a four-bedroom house on 4 hectares in River Road, Millstream, a general-store one-pub 1200-resident rural town on the river of the same name in the rugged Tablelands Region 125 km south-west of Cairns. They paid $107,000 for it and sold four years later for $235,000.

For Gareth and the two children, at least at first, the ensuing years involved following Stacey from one teaching gig to the next. The first published and dated information recording Madelyn and Aidan, in their mid-and-early teens respectively, were living away from their mother and step-father is from 2012 where Aidan attended'a state school in north-west Queensland'.[2] As no-one in Camooweal mentioned any Train children, it is likely Madelyn and Aidan were away earlier and avoided association with Gareth's bizarre actions and reputation there.

Gareth and Stacey's next property purchase was made when they lived in Mt Isa in 2013. They paid $50,000 for 44 hectares at Kumbarilla in the Western Downs, traditionally a freehold grazing area. On the vast Surat Basin Jurassic coalbed, methane 'traps' abound and fracking opportunities exist. The Train's property only makes economic sense as a speculative investment for fracking, either by selling to QGC or Origin or Santos, or by royalties paid by them to frack on the place. The nearest school is Tara Shire State College, which is where Stacey got a gig six years later. (They sold Kumbarilla for $62,000 in 2021.)

Two years after buying the gas land, they bought 251 Wains Road Wieambilla. Sometime around when Stacey got the Tara College gig in 2019, the pair moved in.

* * *

The fortification of 251 was the work of Gareth Train. A previous resident called the house and grounds 'normal'. Madelyn reported Gareth liked reading books on military matters, and that he had at onetime considered a military career.

Logs ready to be rolled out to block vehicles. Barbed wire. Foxholes. A bunker. Steel barricades. Mirrors high on trees for surveillance. Security cameras. Tripwires and sensors on approaches to the house connected to an indoor alarm. Dirt mounds. Kill zones. This is all straight from the doomsday prepper/sovereign citizen handbook, which itself leans heavily on modern infantry tactics. This Troy-on-the-Western-Downs would be comic if three tragic murders had not gone down there.

* * *

My best shot at understanding the three killers' individual ease at killing people, Rachel, Matthew and Alan, none of who had ever done them a bad turn, is that to them, representatives of law enforcement or concerned neighbours didn't matter a fig. They were mere pawns, symbols, collateral damage. Inside the kill team, before that awful day, Gareth would refer to other people as 'soulless, spiritless meat suits'. The big picture looks to be that the crazy religious and political ideas that they held in common, allowed them to kill righteously, die as heroes and assuredly rise from the dead in due course.

1 Rory Callinan & others, ABC News, 15 December 2022

2 'Tracking the Trains', *Daily Mail Australi*a, 5 March 2023; https://www.qatsif.org.au/stories/2018/4/16/qatsif-student-aidan-train-named-as-2015s-highest-achiever

6
The Wieambilla Blocks

'We [Blockies] are considered the Negroes the Western Downs... They [farmers, Tara townspeople] are the ones who avoid us. They have a fear of us, and reaction to fear is aggressiveness. They have always been suspicious about the people living in the Blocks. And we are the outsiders as we were not born here.'
– Michael, Blockie

'The town would have died if people from the Blocks did not help us; the people who were never welcomed by the town.'
– George, a Tara business owner

'Wieambilla' is a local district name derived from the old name of the creek, or an old grazing run, or a parish – no-one is now sure – on the Western Downs in south-west Queensland.

The Downs have good soils for growing grains to the east and good grazing land in its west, but the soils of Wieambilla have nothing for a whitefella farmer and have defeated the agronomists who have visited it. Only the members of the tough brigalow suite of trees and shrubs thrive there, enjoying the lack of botanical competition.

The first Australians on the Downs were the Barrunggam people, speaking Barrunggam.

Ludwig Leichhardt 'explored' the area. The first numerically significant whitefella settlement of the Downs came in the decade of the 1910s. They were mainly Victorians who sailed to Brisbane, took the train for 300 km to Dalby and went west with horse teams to found places like Tara, today only a $3^1/_2$ hour's drive from Queensland's capital city. They ring-barked and felled the brigalow and wattle, sowed European grasses wherever seeds took, bought and bred sheep, and wool became king. It took time, but the God of Prosperity followed and, it seemed, moved in.

Wieambilla, 20 km from Tara, growing ironbark, cypress pine and paperbark scrub, was unsuitable for sheep grazing and was pretty much skipped by development and prosperity.

The geology of Wieambilla is of river sediments laid down in the Permian and Triassic periods – the boundary between the two is 250 million years old, very ancient for surface rocks. Over those years it had been buried and compressed by deposits of later sediments now gone. It never had the benefit of the weathered old lava flows or runoff from those lava flows which weather to a fertile trace-element-rich soil. Hundreds of millions of years had done its damage. The result is an inch of poor soil, a yard of hard clay and rock like concrete as one digs down.

The Downs is part of the 'Brigalow Belt' of Queensland and northern NSW, a temperate region that favoured plants which could deal with low rainfall, high evaporation and tolerate clay and salt, like *Acacia harpophylia* aka brigalow. Once, brigalow forest covered vast areas but 90 percent has been cleared. The paradise parrot was last seen in 1927. The marsupial rabbit-rats and hopping-mice too are now extinct. The remanent belt's conservation status is 'critical/endangered'.

* * *

The origin of the Wieambilla blocks lie in poor government planning and the failure of Soldier Settlement schemes.

The area was surveyed, and divided into small blocks of open, scrubby bushland earmarked for returned soldiers after World War 1. The ex-soldiers never did settle on them, but the surveyors left a legacy: 2000 or so blocks with legal freehold title just waiting for a buyer, arguably for a mug. Some, called 'spaghetti blocks', were just 300 metres wide roadside but 1.5 km deep. More typically, the blocks were around 15 hectares – 37 or 38 acres – though some were 10, others 40 or more hectares.

The ex-soldiers did not come in 1919, but the feral cactus prickly-pear did. These two things look related. Where prickly pear grew, it put out roots which produced shoots, result cactus jungle; fallen seed-laden fruit was spread by animals, result the speedy spread of the cactus jungles. On the Western Downs generally, growing a radish for a salad was hard, and growing wool near impossibly tough.

The introduction of the *cactoblastis* moth six years later under the management of the Commonwealth Scientific and Industrial Research Organisation, CSIRO, turned that tide around. The Chinchilla Memorial Hall sings the moths' praises today. In nearby Miles a Rhyl Inwood sculpture of a prickly pear stem with the CSIRO's paper tubes of moth eggs twisted both ends for the public to spread among the cactus stands was unveiled in 1985 with a plaque reading, in part, 'This represents the most successful conquest of a plant pest by biological control in the world's history – a tribute to scientific endeavour'.

Prosperity was back on the Western Downs. It did not last long.

The area was hit hard by drought, then the collapse of the Australian Wool Reserve Price Scheme and the global wool industry downturn in the 1990s. In the towns and townships like Dalby, Moonie, Condamine, Miles, Chinchilla, Tara and others, residents read the signs: the shuttered shops, falling school enrolments, businesses for sale and obviously few takers, a disinclination to spend money on house paint and the like… Those signs still exist in the 2020s.

In the 1960s and 1970s the Wieambilla blocks were – and still are – marketed by Washington Developments Pty Ltd. They were sold off cheap, $35,000 then, $50,000 now are typical, to interested people seeking alternative lifestyles out of town. Once, deposits were a mere $100 or $200.

The roads are unsealed. A key one here, Wains Road, is fine after trucks drop off quarried gravel and the Shire grader has gone over it, but it reverts to a gravelled dusty, rutted, weedy track in time. Storms and surface water can render roads impassable for days. Drone vision of the turnoff into Wains Road used by TV journalists excluded from the kill site in the summer of 2022-23 and used as background in their reports, showed a straight-as-a-ruler well-kept red-gravel road.

Most blocks are not connected to sewerage, water supply or electricity systems. Septic plumbing systems, drop toilets and fences are difficult to build: the bedrock is hard and close to the surface. Port-a-loos and rainfall-collection tanks often must suffice. Some people still prefer candlelight and lanterns, but modern, affordable solar panels have been a boon for most. Telstra is the sole operator of mobile phone coverage there, but residents report that black spots occur when storms break and calls often drop out. Although Wieambilla sits on the Surat Basin, part of the Great Artesian Basin, bore water is difficult to tap. Hence, few blocks are on bore water or fully fenced. As at 251 Wains Road, shallow dams generally hoard water but these run dry in droughts. The Tara Shire State College provides toiletry kits and showers to students who have to do without water at home.

The 'Blockies' – some rejoice in the moniker, others prefer 'landowner', and there is no dodging the social stigma often intended or implied by the word's users; 'ferals' too is used – are a diverse lot. Asthma sufferers like the clean low-humidity air. Retired workers applaud being far from the madding crowd. Tree changers. People looking to be self-sufficient: goat faming on the side in the 1990s was popular. Old hippies and their middle-aged offspring on the bong can grow their own and sell a bit for cash. Veterans seek healing from post-traumatic stress disorder. Some are workers who commute 45 minutes to Tara. Some Blocks are really weekenders and hobby farms, city-siders' second properties.

Since the shootings, attention has naturally been drawn to the right-wing conspiracy theorists with guns, unlicensed ones, there. There has been talk that para-military training camps are held on some Blocks, though it is, at the time of writing, still just talk.

Nevertheless, driveway gates with signs like these are common:

BEWARE OF THE DOGS
Keep out
Trespassers will be prosecuted
SURVEILLANCE CAMERAS ON SITE

Privacy and property rights are valued greatly. Not knowing your neighbours' names is common.

Actual crime rates on the Wieambilla Blocks are high. The Blocks are in the Tara Police District near the border of the Chinchilla beat. Tara recorded 1040 offences in 2021 and 2022: 232 drug, 167 theft, 118 property damage, assault and 92 unlawful entry offences made up most of these. To underscore Wieambilla's contribution, Queensland Police published a cluster map of crimes reported in the two beats in those years. In the nature of such things, most crimes cluster where most of the people are, in and around Chinchilla with over 7000 and Tara with nearly 2000. Nevertheless, sparsely populated Wieambilla is a stand-out for third place. It is not much of a stretch to ascribe much of it to cannabis growing and use, and to incidents arising from dope theft, debts and deals gone sour which do not count as drug offences.

It has been said that the Wieambilla Blocks produced methamphetamine, ice in the 1980s,[1] but that was the boom time of the clandestine lab all over Australia, isolated locales favoured because of the tell-tale odour generated by the process.

Block housing includes caravans, tents, dongas (temporary, moveable dwellings), and shipping containers. Some are temporary, to be lived in while the householder builds more comfortable, better housing. Some are how the owners choose to live, rough but ready.

* * *

Once, there was not a lot of asset appreciation in owning a Block. That changed, dramatically so in spots, around the mid-2010s when Shell started buying up blocks as sites for drill rigs, pipe pathways and pumping stations to extract coal-seam gas.[2] Some blocks are worth as little as $1,500, while next door there are properties worth up to $2 million, owned by coal seam gas company QGC.[3]

When police set up an exclusion zone after the 12 December shootings one roadblock was under a sign:

HIGH PRESSURE
BURIED GAS PIPELINE

This methane-extraction boom did not really bring in more people. QCS established temporary work camps to build the holding ponds of water, compressor stations and gas wells needed. These camps were parks of large caravans, often housing more than 100 workers. The Wieambilla Blocks and the area around Tara have largely escaped gas developments so far, pipe-laying aside, but many say gas is the future and it is coming.

Environmentalists and blockies worry about adverse effects on their water supplies. Operators have brine collection ponds and they desalinate the water they use, but heavy-metal contamination is a worry.

Some farmers have reported bad experiences when 'the frackers' were on or had left their land, promises not kept, stock control made impossible, and years spent in civil litigation to get compensation. Residents, blockies included, have blockaded gas workers' camp exits, bringing their work to a standstill, and minor altercations have been known.[3]

Passions run high as they always do when a risk of contamination of drinking water is in the thinking. The alliance of Lock-the-gate famers and reclusive blockies in protest is perhaps not as unlikely as the Akubra-meets-beanie stereotypes suggest. Water is life for native and sown vegetation, native and feral wildlife, game, farm animals and pets. And for people.

The 2021 Census put the population of Wieambilla as 78, but some people there clearly prefer not to be counted. Firefighters and others fighting bushfire outbreaks there figured the local electoral rolls greatly underestimated the blockies' numbers. Social-science researchers doing fieldwork in these blocks in 2013 estimated around 3000 people lived there.[4]

The local government area is the Western Downs Regional Council, headquartered in Dalby. The WDRC was created by a deeply unpopular amalgamation of old shires. It is the size of Tasmania, nearly that of Switzerland. Politically, it had long been the safe National Party seat of Maranoa, now a Liberal-National Party seat held by David Littleproud MP, a Chinchilla lad, a cabinet minister in the Turnbull Government, and Minister of Agriculture, Drought and Emergency Management in the Morrison one. Likewise, the State seat of Warrego is a very safe LNP seat. That safety, as usual in safe seats in hard times, has been blamed for the perceived lack of interest in Canberra and Brisbane, for being the reason for the area's people, communities, facilities, economies and – what else have you got? – being taken for granted.

* * *

After the murders of 12 December but before Deputy Commissioner Tracy Linford's assurance backed by ASIO to the public that the Trains were an autonomous cell, a one-off, so there were no associates to worry about and public safety was assured, journalist Candace Sutton found a block that might be worth worrying about.

Independently, the respected Tara local David Maynard had gone there too, taken photos of the block and handed them over to police at the wake for Rachel and Matthew at the Tara cop shop. Tara townies recalled guys in camouflage gear getting out of their camo-painted prime-mover truck to shop.

New Zealander Jessee Wood, a blond and bearded smoker of fat cigars with a fine barber, bought the 100-hectare (250-acre) South Road block in February 2021, high-pandemic time, for $150,000. The place is 20 minutes on the road from 251 Wains Road. If you trust his Facebook account, Wood is the CEO of Kiwi Guy Enterprises, Kiwi Guy Computers, a big wheel in Hydra Corp Industries, and in 420 Fanatics who, under their marijuana-leaf logo, have a head-shop/tobacconist/vape shop in Brisbane. He mentioned Elysium Security as an associate but the French cyber-security firm said it had no presence, no agents and no clients in Australia or New Zealand.

What bought this block to media, community and in the wake of Trains' killings, police attention, was the 360-degree cameras installed, heaps of military sourced camo-painted dongas, and judging from street signs 'Pioneer' and 'First', the presence of many undocumented people. There was no permanent dwelling on the property and no paperwork existed to suggest there would ever be one. They'd erected a decent 7-metre or so flag pole. It flew a New Zealand flag with an Australian one underneath, but no Aboriginal flag at all. On the face of things, it had all the hallmarks of a 'terrorist training camp'.

Journo Sutton either visited the joint or sent in an operative to jack up an interview. No go. A man leashed to an eager pitbull, a terrier-bulldog cross braying from the depths of its ancestry, headed them off at the gate. He told them the business of the joint was 'security' and all those dongas were 'staff accommodation'.

Jessee Wood has stated 'we do not share the same ideals' with respect to the Trains. Sure. What he is silent on, is what ideals he, deep in the Condamine State Forest, does have. Clearly, Queensland Police raiders found no unlicensed weapons or explosives, illicit drugs, or people with warrants out on them, as no charges have followed. Jessee Wood's interview by police was lengthy.[5]

* * *

The new 'crop' of the Western Downs is energy. It dwarfs all else.

The Moonie Oilfield, Australia's first commercial oilfield, on the Surat Basin, was discovered and developed in the 1960s. Production peaked in 1966. The last two of 38 wellheads were built in 1981. Millions of barrels of crude oil were produced. It is still producing, although the field is 'watered out'. Gas from the oilfield saw a pipeline to Brisbane built in the 1960s for domestic and industrial use, but the line was decommissioned in 2008 following a shutdown after a leak in a Brisbane suburb was discovered. Gas extraction – now coal-seam gas, or CSG – from the Surat Basin has spread far beyond Moonie, nudging Wieambilla among other Western Downs places.

QGS, a subsidiary of Shell plc of London, and operated by Shell, has joined with PetroChina and Tokyo Gas as, in corporate-speak, 'development partners.' Arrow Energy Holding Pty is an incorporated joint venture of Shell and PetroChina. Drill rigs, pipe pathways and pumping stations went in and coal-seam gas was drawn out of the rock.

Coal-seams undergo hydraulic fracture – water, sand and chemicals are pumped under pressure into the seams, cracks and fissures. In Australia chemicals are heavily licenced and hardly used, but fracturing the seam under hydraulic pressure can have other impacts, including on groundwater quality by cross connection of aquifers.

Relief of gas pressure by removing some of the groundwater allows the gas to separate from the water and rise to the well head. The gas is piped to compressors and, eventually, after cooling to a liquid state – an Australian technological first – to tankers in coastal ports as liquefied natural gas, LNG, for export.

The water removed is typically salty. It is piped to holding ponds and water treatment stations for desalination. The Kenya Water Treatment Plant in Chinchilla supplies town drinking water, and water for agricultural irrigation.

The sand, in engineering-speak is a 'proppant'. It keeps natural and stimulated fractures in the coal seams 'propped' open. The chemicals are lubricants, germicides, anti-rust agents, binders to salts, and a host of others.

Coal Seam Gas, CGS, products are set to be second only to iron ore as an Australian export earner soon, displacing coal. With war in the Ukraine and Russian gas embargoed, exports in 2022-23 are predicted to peak at $90 billion, then experience a fall in price but greater volumes. (Coal exports are predicted to be $120 billion and to fall in volume.)[6]

But petroleum gas is not the only energy generator on the Downs.

Diamond Energy has 61,000 panels on a sun-tracking system dubbed 'The Baking Board' there. It will generate 19.9 Megawatts when completed. Work started in 2019, and it is already generating electricity.

The biggest solar farm in Australia, 'The Western Downs Green Power Hub', costing $540 million, is being built 20 kilometres southeast of Chinchilla. First Solar Australia is spending $109 million on its 300-hectare Chinchilla solar photo-voltaic park. It will generate 100MW – enough for 40,000 homes – from 2024. Neoen, a French company billed as a 'renewables giant', has negotiated land use, jobs and job-training matters with local Barrunggam mobs.

It intends to link the hub to the world's largest battery, the Hornsdale Power Reserve, run by Tesla, in South Australia. Neoen plans to generate 400 Megawatts, enough to power 220,000 homes.

* * *

Gareth and Stacey Train bought their 45-hectare Wieambilla block in 2015 for $96,000.[7]

Stacey did what household shopping needed doing in Tara where she had the teaching job at Tara Shire State College. A sighting of Gareth in Tara was as rare as a sighting of the grey range thick-billed grasswren. The covid pandemic of 2019, the year of Gareth's first known mad-as-a-snake conspiracy post, hit Queensland the following year. The Palaszczuk Government of Queensland responded. Stacey, like Gareth, was staunchly against vaccination. Citing that reason, to dodge the jab, she quit her job that year. From then on, she lived her days almost entirely with only her domineering husband for company. Then, Gareth's brother, her ex-husband Nathaniel, joined them.

On Tara's main street during the pandemic, a conspiracy theorist like Gareth could be forgiven for thinking the force was with him. A big black sign there with hand-painted slogans exhorted viewers to 'stand up for freedom', join 'the peoples' revolution' to stop Australia becoming 'a dictatorship'.[8]

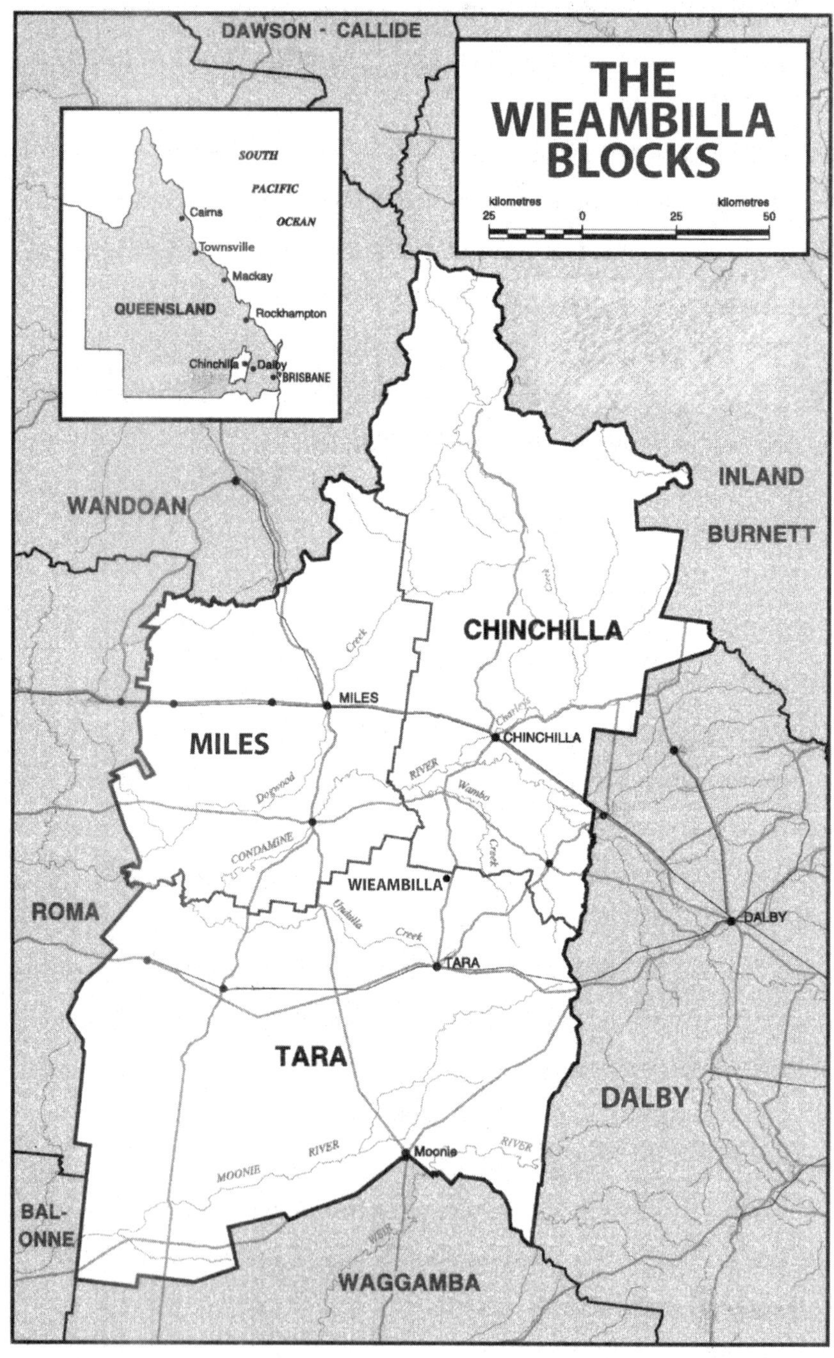
THE WIEAMBILLA BLOCKS
kilometres
25
0
25
kilometres
50
DAWSON - CALLIDE
SOUTH
PACIFIC
OCEAN
Cairns
Townsville
Mackay
QUEENSLAND
Rockhampton
Chinchilla
Dalby
BRISBANE
WANDOAN
INLAND
BURNETT
CHINCHILLA
MILES
MILES
CHINCHILLA
ROMA
WIEAMBILLA
DALBY
TARA
TARA
DALBY
Moonie
MOONIE
RIVER
RIVER
BAL-
ONNE
WAGGAMBA

That covid restrictions have fuelled a bizarre set of anti-government reactions online, on the streets and in some corners of traditional media outlets in many of the world's democracies is no secret. The anti-vaxx and anti-pandemic restrictions words on placards among the civilians who stormed the US Capitol, for example, is plain for all the world to see. Many of the slogans and symbols displayed there were seen in protests here, from Perth to Townsville.

On the Western Downs it has also seen many Wieambilla blocks snapped up by a new type of buyer, a new type of refugee, one spooked by the covid-19 pandemic experience.

1 Liz Hayes, Under Investigation, Nine Now, 15 March, March 2023; and panellist John Coyne, Australian Strategic Policy Institute

2 David Chen and Nibir Khan: 'On Wains Road…' ABC Southern Queensland

3 *Cairns Post*, 21 May 2013

4 Muhammad Makki and Kitty van Vuure, 'Place, identity and stigma: blocks and the "blockies" of Tara, Queensland, Australia, *GeoJournal* (2017) 82:1085-1099 Springer Science+Business Media Dordrecht

5 Candace Sutton, 'Exclusive: inside the strange army-style compound with a camouflaged truck and intense security near the site of the doomsday cult police shooting that has locals spooked – as cops grill owner for hours', *Daily Mail Australia*, 11 January 2023

6 Department of Industry, Science and Resources, 'Australia's resource and energy exports to reach $450 billion', 4 October 2022

7 Candace Sutton, *Daily Mail Australia* 14 December 2022

8 Sarah Krasnostein, 'The Train Family Murders', *The Monthly*, May 2023; Joe Hinchcliffe and *Guardian Australia*

7
The Mad Worlds of Conspiracy Theorists

Conspiracy theory: the theory that an event or phenomenon occurs as a result of a conspiracy between interested parties; spec. a belief that some covert but influential agency (typically political in motivation and oppressive in intent) is responsible for an unexplained event.
– Oxford English Dictionary

A brown root rot never seen before devastates the crop? There's too much impurity in our world, so cut the throat of a virgin on the altar. Villagers finding huge lumps growing on their neck, groin and armpit? Burn more witches. Conspiracy theories go way back. The Enlightenment, the march of reason, the spread of education and scientific progress, rolled lots of such theories back, but many have proved reason-resistant and able to take new forms.

The d.o.b. of the world-wide web is forever arguable, but 1991 is a favourite, bets on Sir Tim Berners-Lee, at CERN in Switzerland at the time. A lot of comments online forget that the web did not create conspiracy theories. People do. However, it provided the platform for direct access to the eyes and ears of an audience. The gatekeepers of government, media and technology with their laws, standards, economics, reputations, traditions and rules were circumvented. The upsurge of conspiracy-centred explanations of the way the world worked that happened in the late 20th and early 21st centuries suggest the world wide web is the reason why. There are no other contenders.[1]

The Covid-19 pandemic experience has super-charged interest in conspiracy theories. Not directly relevant to the Wieambilla shooters, but the maddest out-there and best documented nonsense I know of, is QAnon . Early QAnon believers were sure that the US government was, and had been for a long time, controlled by an elite cabal of Satan-worshipping paedophiles, the Illuminati. Sometimes 'the Jews' or Hilary Clinton were said to be central to it. Sometimes they also ate babies. Believers tend to think it was the CIA, not Lee Harvey Oswald, a mere patsy, who killed President John Kennedy; that the 9/11 attacks were inside jobs; and that covid-19 was not a virus but a government hoax. During the coronavirus restrictions, hashtag analysts saw QAnon activity on Facebook jump 700 per cent.

The story of one of the world's best known and most heavily studied forgeries, 'The Protocols of the Elders of Zion', illustrates key features of conspiracy theories. A Russian Orthodox mystic working with Tsarist police wrote about the Coming of the Antichrist during some anti-Jewish pogroms in Russia in 1902-3. He included 'The Protocols' as the minutes of a meeting of world Jewish leaders who were organising world domination via 24-point plan: to subvert the morals of gentiles, have Jews take over the banks, the press... No names, no date, no venue. In fact, he mashed it up from bits of a French political satire and an anti-Jewish German novelist's works and made it all up. He used 'we' and 'us' forms, not 'I' and 'you', a common presumption among propagandists. He adds truisms no-one would dispute. He uses generalisations without illustration or examples. After the 1917 communist revolution, some fleeing Russians used 'The Protocols' to explain the Big Picture: the

Bolsheviks were the Jews carrying out world domination. Flexibility is inherent in conspiracy theories: enemies can be made to suit.

Hitler read a German edition and wrote 'we are told they are based on a forgery as the *Frankfurter Zeitung* moans every week… the best proof that they are authentic… the important thing is that with terrifying certainty they reveal the nature and expose their inner contexts as well as their ultimate final aims.'[2] Hitler's dismissal of mainstream media, MSM in on-line conspiracist circles, is an enduring feature. Henry Ford was a believer and re-published The Protocols, until forced to retract. Books based on it still sell in the Middle East and Japan, though no-one (except for a single British conspiracy-theorist) publishes it in the West.

Today, 'The Protocols of the Elders of Zion' – known to be a total fiction for 100 years – is rolling again, in new clothes, on the Internet. Blatant anti-Jewish stances are deemed a bit uncool, so the Jews become The Illuminati and/or Freemasons, or rich Jews like the Rothschild family or George Soros, along with a sprinkle of cosmopolitan gentiles intent on 'destroying the [white, unsaid but understood] nation', figures the theorists don't like, just to muddy the waters a bit, or just 'Zionists'.[3]

The FBI posted an automated Twitter bot linked to a 139-page file with the key Protocol text on the web. 'Hate-filled praise' streamed back, far exceeding sceptical or rebutting comment.[4] #zionistagenda, #israhell and #saturndeathcultkiller are two obvious supporters, and the last an insider's antisemitic code.

An off-duty cop, Brandon Mendoza, was killed in a head-on collision with a vehicle driven by an unlicensed, very drunk, undocumented immigrant using the wrong side of the road in Mesa, Arizona in 2014.

His mother, Mary Ann Mendoza, told candidate Donald Trump her story and how she was joining with other victims of crimes in the Angel Families movement, in which she became known as 'Angel Mom'. She appeared on a panel show with Trump, was a guest speaker at the

Republican National Convention in 2016 and at Immigration Forums in 2019 alongside Nick Fuentes, a self-labelled racist, sexist, Holocaust-denying, antisemitic raver. She worked for President Trump, establishing his Victims of Immigration Crime Engagement office. And she was due to be a guest speaker at the Republican National Convention in 2020.

Her appearance was abruptly dropped from the line-up of events when news surfaced of her Tweet on MAM@mendoz480 to her 40 000 followers with links referencing 'The Protocols' and attacking the Rothschild family and George Soros who, Protocols style, were planning to enslave the goyim.

The case of Mary Ann Mendoza serves to remind us that thinking dangerous conspiracy theorists are folk living up a gully in some 'Deliverance country' somewhere, is – besides being a common urban bigotry of its own – just wrong. Ms Mendoza was intelligent, socially skilful, telegenic, energetic, persuasive, eloquent and successful. She seized opportunities and came to wield considerable national moral and political influence.

That conspiracists are not all intellectual midgets who are socially isolated failures does not mean they are not dangerous. Quite the contrary.

* * *

A family friend of the former prime minister of Australia, Tim Stewart or on Twitter @BurnedSpy34, was a QAnon cultist. Tim and Lynelle Stewart's and Scott and Jenny Morrison's friendship went back to their twenties. They worshipped at the Maroubra Baptist Church. The two men went to rugby-league games to cheer on the Cronulla Sharks.

Tim had long been interested in odd internet conspiracies, but after around 2015, he started talking about a 'secret banking system', made friends with a Gold Coast True Blue Crew neo-nazi and a Hollywood actor who claimed to be blowing the whistle on US film-industry paedophiles. These friends were houseguests at the Stewarts' place, sitting around watching posts about, or discussing satanic rituals, many involving the rape and killing of children.[5]

When Alexander Downer, a former minister for foreign affairs and Australia's high commissioner to the UK, met with George Papadopoulos, a foreign-policy specialist on candidate Donald Trump's election advisory panel, in a London bar in May 2016 they discussed Trump's chances. Papadopoulos said the Russians 'might release some information which could be damaging' to Hilary Clinton, Trump's Democratic Party rival for the presidency and then leading in the polls. Downer felt he should share this oddity – a role for Russians in a US election was then truly an oddity – with Australian intelligence.

When Wikileaks published over 19 000 emails that someone had hacked from the Democratic National Committee records in July 2016, Australian intelligence figures felt their American counterparts should know about what Papadopoulos said to Downer. The FBI launched an investigation into possible Russian interference.

Trump supporters got busy denigrating Downer, and dug for dirt on him. QAnon cultists did too. @BurnedSpy34 joined them. He made a link to a 1996 inquiry into accusations of child sexual abuse by foreign ministry staffers and diplomats in Asian nations. Downer was Minister for Foreign Affairs when the inquiry opened; the alleged offences were said to have occurred long before Downer got that job. The link was clearly spurious but Tim Stewart sailed into it: 'It's no coincidence that Downer did NOT want Trump elected.' Conspiracy theorists have little interest in coincidence when it gets in the way of a dark plot, and they so adore outing paedophiles, they see them everywhere. Another ex-foreign minister, Julie Bishop, was in on it too: her red shoes a complete giveaway, worn to hide the blood on the ground when children are being slaughtered. Eventually, @BurnedSpy34's account on Twitter was permanently suspended for Tim Stewart's 'engaging in harmful activity'.

By late 2019 the *Guardian Australia* was questioning PM Scott Morrison's personal judgement. ALP Senator Penny Wong used an Estimates Committee hearing to ask if Lynelle Stewart was on the Prime Minister's Sydney house staff? Had a QAnon conspiracy theorist been invited to the PM's residences? Lynelle was indeed on the payroll, and Tim had indeed visited. However, the PM said, 'I find it deeply offensive that there would be any suggestion that I would have any involvement or support for such a dangerous organisation; I clearly do not.'

In 2018 PM Morison delivered an apology on behalf of the nation to victims of crimes uncovered by a royal commission into institutional responses to child sexual abuse. He said, 'The crimes of ritual sexual abuse happened in schools, churches, youth groups, scout troops, orphanages…'

A blogger with a special interest in conspiracy theories noted that the term 'ritual sexual abuse' was, to QAnon and like readers and listeners, shorthand for satanic elites raping children in tunnels under Washington DC pizza joints or in Hollywood. The blogger noted the phrase was picked up by some of the usual suspects he knew, like @StormIsUponUs: 'The new Prime Minister of Australia must be a rider in #TheStorm. Here he is making an unprecedented statement on the cabal-engineered epidemic of child ritual abuse.' (The blogger wrote that Morrison may have used 'ritual' to simply mean *systematic* or *methodical.* In the context of the royal commission report, the grubby offences lacked the solemnity and gravity usually conjured up by 'ritual'.)

Crikey! journalist David Hardaker wrote 'Scott Morrison's conspiracy-theorist friend claims he has the PM's ear – and can influence what he says'. @BurnedSpy34 was outed as Tim Stewart then and traced back:

On the day Morrison took office: 'A fresh start. Rebuilding a new identity.'

On the passing of harsher mandatory sentencing laws: 'Australia has had notoriously short sentences for pedo's.'

On the national apology speech above: 'A new conversation began today in Australia. It was a stepping stone to be sure, but we took the step. @ScottMorrisonMP took control of the narrative powerfully and commenced phase 1 of our restoration.'

Hardaker also dug out some Facebook posts by the Stewarts' old Gold Coast True Blue Crew neo-Nazi house guest. He was no longer a pal of Tim's; he was an angry and vengeful man. He had a crackpot theory about an Australian bank which had collapsed at the end of the 1970s, and he believed the bankers had hidden US$15 trillion – far more than the US's entire Gross Domestic Product in 1980. He had wanted Tim to get his pal Scott to investigate the bank and Tim wouldn't or couldn't.

So, he spilled the beans on Facebook about what Tim had confided to him personally. That Tim was going to get Scott to use 'ritual sexual abuse' in the national apology speech. And quoted Tim: 'Think of this like code that sends a direct and clear message that they have been heard by Scott specifically.' On the big day, 'I think Scott is going to do it. Pretty sure speeches at 11. I hope he says it. Scott is very aware of the enormity of today.'

Tim however publicly held to his line that he had 'never spoken to Scott about anything of a political nature'.

The blogger specialist suggested the Prime Minister may have figured it was good electoral politics to signal to the smarties in the conspiracy cult world that he was with them. The phrase would be lost in space for others. So, an ambiguous, deniable use had no downside. The PM may well have known that @BurnedSpy34 had over 21 000 followers. The mysterious, revered Q had previously blessed @BurnedSpy34 simply by commenting favourably on a thread he wrote. Thus anointed, Tim Stewart's following was made. On the platforms he used, like 8chan, he was considered 'world class'.

Politicians tend to be good at numbers, influence and power implications.

* * *

It is pointless to debate with conspiracy theorists. Never wrestle with pigs. You both get dirty, and the pig likes it. Such theories are based in emotional conviction, and subject to blind faith. Debate admits the possibility of proving something false. Conspiracy theories, by definition, are irrefutable.

These theorists' circular reasoning means that the evidence against (and the absence of evidence for) equals evidence of its truth. They see cover-ups everywhere. They need cover-ups – nudge, nudge, wink, wink – for the gaps in their 'logic'. Their shadowy villainous conspirators are *always* good at covering their tracks and duping people. Debate is effectively blocked by 'They want you to think that.'

These people distrust academics, scientists, historians and, particularly, journalists. Psychologists note that conspiracy theories appeal disproportionally to people with paranoid and/or narcissistic personalities or conditions – those with a sense of persecution and/or holding an inflated sense of self. Many reflect feelings of resentment, indignation and disenchantment with the world.

The stories these conspiracies tell are of good and absolute evil; there is little or no room for grey. An apocalyptic strain, a belief in an imminent confrontation between good and evil, is very common. Because of their strong emotional attachments to these stories – so say people who *must* talk to conspiracy theorists – fact countering is seldom useful; better to ask, 'Why is that?' and 'Who is behind that?'

The number of those who must talk to them is growing apace with the growth of adherents. Friends and family who watch their loved ones spending heaps of time on conspiracy websites and in online chatrooms worry. They fear, as they commonly put it, the loved one going further 'down that rabbit hole', wasting their lives and opportunities, spending time on rubbish with 'sickos', and sprouting (or hiding) weird nonsense, sometimes alarming nonsense.

Worried friends and family look to cult and terrorism deprogrammers, psychologists, police mediators and the like, for tips on how to deal with the conspiracy theorist at their table.

These experienced people all counsel patience. Never lose social contact with the afflicted, they advise.

1 Gregory S Camp, Robert Alan Goldberg and Mark Fenster document this surge and are oft-quoted writers on the phenomenon in the US context

2 *Mein Kampf* [My Struggle], 1925

3 Emma Green Ellis, 'The Internet Protocols of the Elders of Zion', *Wired*, March 2017

4 Steven J Zipperstein, 'The Conspiracy Theory to Rule Them All', *The Atlantic*, 25 July 2020

5 Van Badham, *QAnon and on: a short and shocking history of internet conspiracy cults*, 2021

8
SovCits

Given the matter is still being investigated, I will refrain from going into more detail about ASIO's assessment other than to say we did not find evidence the killers embraced a racist and nationalist ideology or were Sovereign Citizens, despite their anti-authority and conspiracy beliefs. It's disappointing some commentators and self-proclaimed terrorism experts were so quick to make definitive declarations about motivations, ideologies and political alignments in the immediate aftermath of the tragedy.

– Mike Burgess, ASIO Director-General's Annual Threat Assessment, 21 February 2023, on the Wieambilla shootings

Stacey Train was said to have called 251 Wains Road a 'sovereign state', a sovereign citizen position for private land. On the sovereign-citizen and doomsday-prepper websites he visited since 2019, Gareth's posts included how he had spent years building 'an ark… preparing to survive tomorrow'.[1] On such sites 'ark' is understood to be any refuge from whatever mayhem comes, like Noah's ark in The Flood of the Bible. He can only have meant turning 251 Wains into a self-sufficient fortress; he did not build anything else there and seldom left the property.

Despite the censure of the nation's security boss above, the words we know of that came out of 251 Wains Road in the days before the ambush, as we will see in more detail in Chapter 11, echo some of the sentiments, rhetoric and crazy 'values' of the sovereign citizen and doomsday prepper hymn book. Conspiracy theories leak into one another. Borders are not plain.

One example is the Train-written script on one of his Youtube posts 'Stand by my front gate'. A key characteristic of sovereign citizens, henceforth SovCits here, is the sanctity of private property and an extreme, demented concept of what constitutes trespass.

In all the Trains' known ravings Burgess is correct in stating there were no racist or nationalist raves, no suggestion of the alt-right's Great Replacement theory that good white men are being elbowed out by blacks, Asians, immigrants, Muslims or Jews, as some SovCits sites insist is happening. Conspiracy theorists pick and choose from the elements available. The Christchurch mosque shooter choose racist themes but the Trains did not.[2]

The Wikipedia entry on the movement opens a list of associated 'Violent incidents' with the 1995 Oklahoma City bombing, 168 dead, nearly 700 injured. It ends, last update to date, '2022 Wieambilla police shootings'. (Wikipedia also lists shootings of police in Memphis, Tennessee and Baton Rouge, Louisiana in the 2010s.)

The Federal Bureau of Investigations has posted the SovCits as 'domestic terrorists'. In 2015 the NSW Police did too. In 2020 the Victoria Police Commissioner Shane Patton said officers policing coronavirus compliance had been 'forced to smash the windows of cars and pull people out to provide details' after SovCit types had refused to answer questions or show documents.

When Australian Security Intelligence Organisation security boss Mike Burgess issued a warning about covid-19-related radicalisation and extremism, he got a mention on Mrs Yugi girawil's – Gareth Train's account name – on his YouTube channel.

The SovCit's core belief – if a mish-mash of nonsense can be said to have a core – is that laws, rules, taxes, tolls, court orders and vehicle, gun and dog licences etc are illegitimate because the government itself is illegitimate. So, citizens do not have to obey these impositions or obey law or other enforcement officers, and SovCits swear they will not.

Australian SovCit Wayne Glew, ironically an ex-cop, had a Facebook account followed by 10 000 people when I first heard about him six months ago; now, checking in on, that figure is 21,000. This, and his struggles with the Geraldton City Council and in West Australian courts, have made him the nation's best known SovCit. Quoting from the Magna Carta, an 800-year-old English legal document, he argues that he need not pay rates, taxes, legal fees, or obey any law that is imposed on him. For a guy would have delivered a heap of warrants when he was with the police, it is odd to hear him say all the ones he gets are crook: 'photoshopped… incorrect...' The city council, owed $300,000, seized his farm and sold it.

Long-winded, complex ramblings and pseudo-legal arguments are a speciality of SovCits resisting direction by police. The truly committed SovCit is bound to attract police attention: the private vehicles they drive may well not carry registration plates, an offence. The highway patrol officer may be treated to a pedantic distinction between a 'driver' as someone involved in commercial activity who needs numberplates, and a private 'traveller' like them, who does not. Further quibbles about driver's licences can also be expected. In their appearances in US courts, often using the US Constitution in the way that Glew uses the Magna Carta, the roadside argument continues. SovCits tend to represent themselves in courts and tribunals. They practice paper terrorism, firing off filings and motions that quibble over anything and everything, hundreds of pages of drivel essentially. Thus, a straightforward traffic violation can take years to resolve as a result. Courts have responded with systems to nip paper terrorism off at the courthouse door. Legislators have passed laws.

SovCit 'numberplates' available from Amazon, US $22.85 + shipping

In WA Glew has been tagged as a 'vexatious litigant' and 'vexatious prosecutor' to curtail his attempts to exhaust legal process. He has been ordered to pay $2 million in damages to a company that invested in a fuel-supply system he said he was developing. He says he won't pay: the judge is 'corrupt', the penalty legally 'unenforceable'...

But violence, not pettifogging, is our focus here.

In Melbourne during lockdown a policewoman approached a SovCit woman in a shopping centre for not wearing a mask when wearing one was mandatory. The officer was attacked and her head smashed repeatedly on a concrete floor.

* * *

SovCit 'Mrs Yugi girawil' one week before the Wieambilla shootings:

> After dealing with covert agents and tactics for some time now, Daniel

> [Gareth writing as usual in the third person] believes that should they choose to cross the Rubicon with public state actors our Father is giving us a clear sign. Monsters and their heads are soon parted.

Previously, in a rave directed at police and the illegitimate state generally:

> You attempt to abduct us using contractors. You attempt to intimidate and target us with your Raytheon Learjets and planes. You sent 'covert' assets out here to my place in the bush. So what is your play here? To have me and my wife murdered during a state police 'welfare check'? You already tried that one.

'Raytheon' refers to the US aerospace and defence technology company. Raytheon Australia and Air Affairs Australia are involved with the Australian Defence Force, use corporate-marked Learjets for technology testing and training purposes, and early bushfire detection. It is conceivable these aircraft, flying out of RAAF Base Amberley say, were seen by the Trains over the Western Downs, but it only a paranoid and/or narcissistic personality could imagine he or she was their 'target'.

Replying to a Comment from a US Christian conspiracy theorist, Mrs girawil wrote:

> My phone number & front gate seem to have become popular. 'Welfare checks' aka state sponsored murder has started up again.

With the comfort of conspiracy theory to show that the state is an evil fraud, the police Mrs girawil knows are going to come are demonised as murderers. How much self-inflicted delusion did the killers have to feed themselves to smother the knowledge that flesh-and-blood individuals were coming on a first-cab-off-the-rank basis, and are going die by your hand, and that you in your turn will die?

* * *

In the Trains' behaviour on their block, they exhibited some of the traits of another social movement, the prepper or doomsday prepper or survivalist movement, those who prepare, for WSHTF, When Shit Hits The Fan. Some are prepared for TEOTWAWKI, The End Of The World As We Know It, the Great Zombie Apocalypse.

That could be a natural disaster like repeated wild weather events, tsunami, meteorite impact or total eco-system breakdown, or a man-made one like nuclear war, economic collapse, civil war, foreign invasion or a pestilence on a Black Death scale, this last one popular since covid-19 arrived. The Trains, daughter Madelyn said, 'literally believed' covid-19 was the start of the end of the world.

This end-of-the world is a broad church. The Mormon Church has long preached the wisdom of having years' worth of non-perishable food in the larder in preparation for Christ's Second Coming, as that will be preceded by natural and man-made disasters that include famines. Other denominations and sects share this God-sent apocalypse thinking.

Other preppers stress ecological wisdom and self-sufficiency smarts. Those that can, often move to rural areas or mountain retreats, living off the grid, collecting rainwater, growing food, gathering food from wild areas, hunting, fishing and developing handyman and building skills. Others live urban lives but have a BOB, a Bug-Out Bag, permanently packed so they can bug out to their rural retreat. Others prepare to bunker down at home in town. The rule of 3 seems like as-close-to a universal mantra across these different tribes as they have got: humans can survive 3 minutes without air, 3 hours without shelter, 3 days without water, and 3 weeks without food. As a rule-of-thumb that is pretty realistic.

The prepper scene is very male orientated across its spectrum. It got covered in a hugely popular 2011 National Geographic television documentary series, *Doomsday Preppers*. The preoccupation with firearms, ammunition and military practices and paraphernalia among the preppers approached was over the top. That 'zombies' – non-preppers who survive catalysm – will be shot by Dad before they can loot or invade bug-out homes seemed very well covered, but edible mushroom lore, say, much less so. Mum was in the larder with stacks of canned and dehydrated tucker. The cosplay of camo- gear was depressingly evident among those interviewed.

A TV series of six one-hour episodes of the *Last Family on Earth* followed, presumably on the National Geographic doco's high ratings with audiences. This competition reality show involved families vying for a berth in a luxurious state-of-the-art underground bunker. Contestants were judged on their preparedness, skills, aptitude and so on by three 'survivalist experts'.[3] Research has claimed 15 percent of Americans were in the US doomsday market.

* * *

We've seen SovCits like Wayne Glew in action in Australia, but since the Wieambilla Shootings increased attention has been paid to them. Before then, it is highly unlikely a civil and administrative tribunal decision like QCAT's one in R v Nevin Cartwright would have been published beyond the Brisbane tribunal's legislated duties to publish. It made national news: the SovCit and his guns.

In late 2021 Nevin Cartwright went to Rockhampton Police Station. At the front counter, he demanded the officer-in-charge be arrested. A month later he was back, giving the muddle-headed wombats working there the benefit of his wisdom concerning the coronavirus, microbiology and epidemiology. A month after that, QPS Weapons Licensing suspended his firearm licence. He slapped down paperwork for a request for a review seven days later. By late May his licence was revoked. Police decided he was unfit to hold one and noted that his writings showed him to be a SovCit. Cartwright wrote to the state police minister.

Then he went to the Queensland Civil and Administrative Tribunal and treated them to his worldly wisdom, wormed his way out of any suggestion he was a SovCit as SovCits regularly do, and gave the tribunal the benefit of his wisdom concerning the law:

> The statement that I hold sovereign citizen beliefs is indeed an oxy moronic statement as I do not hold them as Queen Elizabeth the second is the sovereign and holder of all lands in The Commonwealth of Australia being that of we the people and I am just a mere share holder of the true Commonwealth of Australia. If you care to read international law it refers to a sovereign and a national never is the citizen-ship (Corpus Juris [body of laws]) of the trust territory under the Hague and UN charter treaties, being that of the Certificate of Birth Registration being a promissory note to fraudulently turn a child into property of the Reserve Bank and bringing that man or women into corpus juris…

The idea that banks secretly buy people at birth as collateral to making loans to governments features in SovCit, QAnon and other conspiracy theories.

> I Nevin-John ask that you issue me with all classes of weapons ownership… I also pray for an open and concealed carry permit as the last act with royal accent (*assent* presumably) was the weapons act of 1973 requiring no licencing for men and women not persons. I Nevin-John ask that a permanent permit to buy be issued with my card that you re-issue as the acts and statutes apply only to legal fictions and as I have left the necromancy.

The tribunal member decided Cartwright's legal argument was 'incomprehensible' so could be ignored, and that anyone who felt the Weapons Act 1990 did not apply to them was clearly 'unfit' to own a gun. In late May 2023 in Brisbane, QCAT upheld the revocation in 2½ pages.[4]

* * *

251 Wains Road Wieambilla, 2022: It is not logical that three people who chose the manner of their doom should be yoked in with people preparing to avoid theirs. But the Trains cherry-picked bits from conspiracy theories that appealed to them – some Christian religious beliefs, 'the state' as persecutors, an anti-vaxx stance – and ignored a lot – the pseudo-legal radicalism underpinning the SovCit movement, racism and nationalism for example. Gareth's raves on-line show him to be a stranger to logic, believing whatever he feels like believing, whatever suits him at the time.

His step-daughter Madelyn Train, in contact with him then by email only then (she visited and stayed with them at mutually convenient times, and ritual times like Christmas, before the epidemic), noticed he had grown obsessed with conspiracy theories and had hardened his anti-government position.

Madelyn thought from what Nathaniel had told her before he went AWOL, that he was taking a break and had gone bush to reconnect with God. She did not know he was at 251 Wains about then. He lied to his daughter. On *A Current Affair* Madelyn's recollection was thus: 'Then they pulled out from society, really… They sorta gave up. Society gave up on them. So they did the same.'[5]

A woman called Margaret rented the homestead at 251 Wains Road for two years in the early 2010s and called the dwelling 'just an ordinary house, four bedrooms, wood on the outside…'[6]

She had heard that, after the Trains moved in, they had lined the walls with steel, barred windows and doors, dug and brick-lined tunnels, added barbed wire and by this bizarre and single-minded reno, turned the house into a fortress. The report or reports Margaret had heard ascribed the tunnelling work (at least) done by a relative of the brothers. As the two brothers had no known contact with family for many years, this rings oddly, but police later found a trapdoor in an internal floor, and a tunnel to outside.

Did they create a fortress to keep people out, but decided later to use it as their base for their last stand?

1 Sarah Kranostein, 'The Train Family Murders', *The Monthly*, May 2023
2 Paul Spoonley & Paul Morris, 'The road to March 15: "networked white rage" and the Christchurch terror attacks', *The Conversation*, 10 March 2023
6 Lacey Rose, 'Spike TV orders Doomsday Survival Competition *Last Family on Earth*', *Hollywood Reporter* 5 June 2013
7 https://www.queenslandjudgments.com.au/caselaw/qcat/2023/168/pdf
8 Aisling Brennan, NCA Newswire, 22 January 2023
9 Candace Sutton, *Daily Mail Australia*, 14 December 2022

9
'Then I saw Thrones...'

We believe in the premillennial, imminent and personal return of our Lord Jesus Christ to gather his people to himself. Having this glorious hope and earnest expectation, we purify ourselves, even as he is pure, so that we may be ready to meet him when he comes.

– End-time clause, Australian Christian Churches, Pentecostal group

The Queensland Police Service broke media silence 66 days after the Wieambilla shootings, a 90-second announcement. Deputy Commissioner Tracy Linford fingered premillennialism as the core belief system that generated the Trains' killing spree. The Service assured the public that there were no associates or fellow travellers arming up, plotting or intending to harm people. The Trains were 'an autonomous cell' who 'acted alone… no evidence… there was [anyone] else involved… [no] ongoing specific threat'. So, relax?

Linford confirmed the Trains had connection to the sovereign citizen movement, referenced Waco 1993, but emphasised 'Christian' and 'religious' extremism as the Trains' prime creed and motivation. Queensland Police investigators had, among other fruits of investigation, access to Stacey Train's diaries, diaries no-one else knew existed.

Meanwhile, Australian journalists were reading more of *The Holy Bible* than they had done before. After all, who can forget the blood-soaked work of Islamic religious extremists, '9/11' front of mind, when they first ventured into translations of *The Holy Koran*?

Premillennialism derives from 200 or so words in the New Testament Book of Revelations 20 1-6:

> 20 Then I saw an angel coming down from heaven, holding in his hand the key to the bottomless pit and a great chain. He seized the dragon, that ancient serpent, who is the devil and Satan, and bound him for a thousand years and threw him into the pit and locked and sealed it over him, so that he would deceive the nations no more, until the thousand years were ended. After that he must be let out for a little while.
>
> Then I saw thrones, and those seated on them were given authority to judge. I also saw the souls of those who had been beheaded for their testimony to Jesus and for the word of God. They had not worshiped the beast or its image and had not received its brand on their foreheads or their hands. They came to life and reigned with Christ a thousand years. (The rest of the dead did not come to life until the thousand years were ended.) This is the first resurrection. Blessed and holy are those who share in the first resurrection. Over these the second death has no power, but they will be priests of God and of Christ, and they will reign with him a thousand years.

John 5, 28-29 is sometimes claimed too: Jesus to Jewish leaders at a temple:

> Do not be amazed at this, for a time is coming when all who are in their graves will hear his voice and come out — those who have done what is good will rise to live, and those who have done what is evil will rise to be condemned.

But that's it for Biblical authority: 260 words in a work of 783,000.

First, say the believers, there will be The Great Tribulation, a period of much hardship, society imploding, 'the End of the World'. Deputy

Commissioner Linford cited the pandemic, climate change and current socio-economic inequality as mentions in Stacey's diaries.

Then, the Second Coming. Christ will return to Earth on a white horse to the sound of trumpets according to some, a far cry from the meek and mild donkey Jesus rode into Jerusalem last time he was here. Satan and unbelievers will be thrown into a Lake of Fire. This heralds the beginning of The Millennium, a 1000-day or a 1000-year (believers vary on this) period of peace and prosperity.

This will end with Judgement Day or, in the premillennialist's favoured name, The Rapture. The Earth's faithful, including those who are dead and who will leave their graves, will rise up and meet God on a cloud.

This belief first surfaced in the 1790s among English Anglican evangelists interested in eschatology, the theology of last things. Those of us, like this author, interested in the history of science, recall that in the medieval period in the West, theology, being about an all-knowing, all-powerful God, was naturally the most important of all branches of thinking and knowledge, dubbed the 'queen of sciences'. Naturally, many of the best young minds were attracted to it; prestige is a magnet. Today, for most, *premillennialism* and *eschatology* are words to put in a search engine to know what whoever is talking or writing about them is on about; unlike, say, nuclear physics or the mathematics of chaos or genetics or black holes... Against the extraordinary advance of modern science, eschatology say, seems like ox-bow lake, a billabong that dried up and shrivelled away to nothing a century or two ago. But premillennialism took root in colonial America among the Plymouth Brethren, and the US has been the base of premillennialism thinking ever since.

Of course, as you my readers will have figured, I think premillennialism is just plain silly. In research for some understanding of the thinking of the Train murderers, I have been amazed to learn how many people believe, adhere, associate by community organisations, churches in particular, and even in their own words, have a total conviction that some sort of doomsday is coming. This conviction is so deep it usually does not need to be stated.

Baptist tele-evangelist Jerry Falwell Sr was a spruiker of this doctrine during the Ford, Reagan and George H Bush administrations. This arch-conservative fulminated from his Lynchburg, Virginia mega-church pulpit. He actively supported the apartheid government of South Africa. He called the Prophet Mohammed 'a terrorist' – but retracted that one. In mid-2006, when the Israeli air force was bombing Lebanon relentlessly, he was asked by CNN's Paula Zahn 'Is the crisis in the Middle East a prelude to the end of the world?'

> I believe in the premillennial, pre-tribulation coming of Christ for all of his church, and to summarize that, your first poll, do you believe Jesus' coming the second time will be in the future, I would vote yes with the 59 percent and with Billy Graham and most evangelicals.[1]

Jerry Falwell Sr's *Old-time Gospel Hour* was regularly viewed by over 50 million. Today the Christian university he founded has 130 000 students in 70 counties, 15 000 of them on-campus in Lynchburg. His moral suasion – the Moral Majority movement was led by Falwell – despite his deeply pro-family beliefs and pronouncements, he helped the divorced Hollywood actor Ronald Reagan defeat the Baptist Sunday school teacher Jimmy Carter in the race to the White House. Falwell's son Jerry Jr, who followed in his father's footsteps in Lynchburg until his sexual peccadilloes were revealed – for years, he was alleged to have enjoyed watching a young pool assistant have sexual congress with his wife – helped randy serial-adulterer Donald Trump similarly. It would be a stretch to say the Rev Falwells were king makers, but they sure helped a lot of The People at polling booths tick Republican candidates in good conscience.

The lesson is that just because premillennialism is an extremely odd belief, that does not mean premillennialists are not powerful and influential. Ex-prime minister Scott Morrison belongs to one of the 1000-odd Pentecostal evangelical churches in the Australian Christian Churches group who subscribe to it.

Most practising Christians get by without giving the end-of-the-world much, if any, thought. Premillennialism is pre-dominantly a Protestant denominational thing, biggest in the American Bible belt, now not as southern a belt as it used to be. Some few Catholics and Orthodox theologians have given it head space. Mormons give it a great deal.

The question here now is how the Train trio came to put this doctrine front and centre of their lives and how such faith drove them to kill and die.

Deputy Commissioner Linford, who I suspect feels as removed from such ancient nonsense and the ruminations of theologians today as I do, was a cop on duty in a press conference. Her first duty is to the community: to preserve the peace and protect life, limb and property. The Trains, said Ms Linford, had in their heads reduced police to 'monsters and demons'. A glance at snapped photos of Racheal, Matthew and Alan make this reduction painfully wrong-seeming, cruel and stupid. Heart breaking. She had been briefed by investigators who have read Stacey's dairies, maybe read them herself. We must wait for the coroner's court to open up on the matter. Her official record of her revelations, 'Investigation Update: Wieambilla shooting event', ends thus:

> If you are aware of someone who is demonstrating suspicious behaviour or are concerned someone is at risk of becoming radicalised, you should report the matter... 1800 123 400 or contact local police.[2]

The key metaphor here is 'rabbit hole'. Australians worried about some child, relation, friend, whatever, first express the misgiving that some loved one or other is going further down some online 'rabbit hole' or other.

* * *

The prevalence of doomsday beliefs is extraordinary. At a ring-wing Christian conference to 'save' the Liberal Party after its election defeat that was held in March 2023 former Queensland Liberal National MP George Christensen said Western culture was possessed by Satan 'literally or metaphorically' and warned civilisation would end in 'our generation unless Christians acted', specifically to flood Liberal Party branches with adherents.

1 CNN transcript 2013-01-16 *Wayback Machine*
2 *My Police: Queensland Police News* 16 February 2023

10
Shooters and Contexts

But the basis of the decision ladies and gentlemen is that we believe that it is in the national interest that there be a dramatic reduction in the number of automatic and semi-automatic weapons in the Australian community... Now, I don't pretend for a moment ladies and gentlemen that the decision that we have taken is going to guarantee that in the future there won't be other mass murders.
– PM John Howard, speech at gun rally,
Sale Victoria, 16 June 1996

The bloodiest peacetime shooting massacre the world had ever seen was the work of a 29-year-old Australian, Martin Bryant, who shot and killed 35 almost randomly selected people at Port Arthur, Tasmania on a day in April 1996. He was not a conspiracy theorist: one must be able to read a bit for that, and reading was beyond his limited intellectual abilities. No religious, political or philosophical inclinations are known. There never was a hint that this social stumblebum loner was a domestic terrorist.

Bryant held that awful record for 15 years, until a 32-year-old Norwegian, Anders Breivik, ignited a car bomb parked outside an Oslo office block where Norway's Labour Party prime minister had his office, killing eight, and, disguised as police officer, travelled to an island where the Workers' Youth League, associated with the Labour Party, were camping, meeting up and chilling out, and shot 69 of them, mostly teenagers, dead, many at point-blank range, on a day in July 2011. He stopped the moment the tactical squad cops arrived, and went into police custody without resistance.

Before he left home to kill that day, he sent his 1500-page manifesto, 2083: A European Declaration of Independence, to 1000 Inboxes and uploaded a 12-minute video on 'the coming Muslim invasion' to YouTube. He was a lapsed member of the anti-immigration Progress Party; in it for seven years until 2006. He joined a pistol club and got a licensed 9 mm Glock. He got a hunting licence and a licensed Ruger Mini-14 rifle. He set up a 'farming' company and followed Timothy McVeigh's recipe for building, planting and detonating a fertiliser-based vehicle bomb. He claimed that day's killings were the result of nine years of planning and organising, including bodybuilding, popping anabolic steroids and videogaming. Breivik has never shown remorse.

Predictably, Breivik did not recognise the court that tried him and was a grandstanding pain-in-the-arse during proceedings, on about how feminism was weakening the white people of Europe and more patriarchy was needed, how Islam and multiculturalism were wrong for Norway, how the Labour Party was complicit... He gave the Nazi salute in court, and in prison found religion in the form of Odinism, a twentieth-century revival of a pre-Christian Scandinavian belief, much fancied by nationalistic and racist conspiracy theorists beyond Scandinavia.

The three-judge bench tried him on specific terrorism charges enshrined in Norwegian statutes – 'destabilising or destroying basic functions of society' and 'creating serious fear in the population', convicted him and handed down the maximum sentence, a kind of renewable 21 years. Besides the practical difficulties of hearing 77 murder charges and other charges relating to the over 300 people he injured, the witnesses were spared somewhat by the invoking of these broad charges.

He acknowledged he had committed the acts, but pleaded not guilty because he acted out of 'necessity'.

Far-right terrorism had certainly shown its hand in Norway in 2011, but Norway is on the other side of the world to Australia. Officially, publicly, far-right terrorism did not raise a blip on Australian law enforcements' radars for another 10 years. Unofficially, who knows?

* * *

In 1992 US Marshals tried to serve an arrest warrant on Randy Weaver of Ruby Ridge, Boundary County, Idaho for his failure to appear in court on firearms charges. The Weaver family had moved there to live off-the-grid, home school their children and escape the corruption of the world that they saw as happening. Randy's wife Vicki led the family's religious beliefs, including that an apocalypse was nigh. Randy refused entry to the marshals. He was holed up in his homestead for 18 months as a result.

A 14-year-old boy, Sammy Weaver, and a young family friend were hunting in the woods for game for the family's table according to the Weavers. US Marshals scouting those woods to find a spot from which they could ambush Randy, hid when they saw the boys, but the Weavers' hunting dog sussed them out. What exactly happened next is unknown but a gunfight ensued, which left Sammy and a marshal dead.

The Federal Bureau of Investigation took over operations on Ruby Ridge. They sent in large numbers of armed-up agents and besieged the home. A sniper shot Vicki dead – she was behind a door that the sniper's target stood in front of it was said. The 11-day siege became a 'circus. Neo-Nazis from the nearby Aryan Nation compound… showed up to protest' and far-rightists poured in to join them, holding signs 'Fed SHOT 1st' and 'YOUR HOME IS NEXT'.[1]

Eventually, Randy Weaver, persuaded by civilian negotiators, agreed to be taken into custody. A suite of federal, state criminal and civil court cases, government departmental inquiries and a Senate subcommittee inquiry followed. The controversy over Ruby Ridge spawned, over the still fairly new-fangled internet, a raft of anti-government organisations like the Oath Keepers, Three Percenters and Light Foot Militia, generally called 'the militia movement'.

* * *

In the following year, the Bureau of Alcohol, Tobacco and Firearms got a warrant to search the Mt Carmel Center Ranch 20 km north-east of Waco, Texas. They carried arrest warrants to be served on David (Lamb of God) Koresh and others of the Branch Davidians who lived in the religious community there. It was thought the cult was stockpiling illegal weapons – they had a licence to make and sell legal weapons and attended gun shows. An article in the *Waco Tribune-Herald* had attacked Koresh's personal morals and behaviour, some of it criminal, the day before the ATF went in:

> If you are a Branch Davidian, Christ lives on a threadbare piece of land 10 miles east of here called Mount Carmel. He has dimples, claims a ninth-grade education, married his legal wife when she was 14, enjoys a beer now and then, plays a mean guitar, reportedly packs a 9 mm Glock and keeps an arsenal of military assault rifles, and willingly admits that he is a sinner without equal.

Entry was denied. A gunfight left four ATF agents and six Davidians dead.

Again, the FBI took charge and there was a siege, this one lasting 51 days and involving Waco police, Texas Rangers, McLennan County Sheriff Department officers, and Texas National Guardsman, using armoured cars, battering rams and Black Hawk helicopters. The siege ended after 51 days when the FBI pitched tear gas canisters into the compound and a fire broke out. The connection or lack of it between these two things became a bone of contention for years afterwards. The fire killed 76 Davidians, including 25 children. Nine walked out.

Many criticisms were levelled at the various authorities involved. One relevant to Wieambilla killers' psychology is that the FBI didn't listen to Biblical scholars and students of apocalyptic cults, who consistently argued that, for Branch Davidians, the confrontation and escalation had cosmic significance and the FBI was reinforcing the apocalyptic ones' determination to fight and die. The Branch Davidians had confidently awaited an apocalypse that heralded the Second Coming of Christ for years. They were premillennials too.

President Bill Clinton was briefed by Attorney-General Janet Reno. She pushed the FBI case for assault on the compound for the following reasons: because children were being sexually abused inside; because a mass suicide was planned; because Linda Thompson, who ran the American Justice Federation, a pro-gun not-for-profit group with militia-movement connections, was said to be going to descend on Waco with her 'Unorganised Militia of the United States'; and because the siege was costing millions. None of the first three reasons ever found back up, and the last, the cost to state coffers, was chickenfeed compared to the legal bills that followed. President Clinton green-lighted her.

The legacy of the Waco Massacre was all downhill. Civil libertarians – of the type dubbed 'snivel libertarians' by the far right to distinguish the lefties from their own, more manly concept of liberty – fumed at the excesses of law enforcement and over-riding of legal process and citizen's rights. This time the far right shared that view, including an ex-Gulf War veteran and militia-movement sympathiser called Timothy McVeigh of Arizona who visited Waco during the siege and again afterwards.

* * *

Timothy McVeigh, with help from an old army buddy, Terry Nichols, another survivalist, white supremacist and anti-government schemer, built a very large bomb of ammonium nitrate fertiliser, nitromethane and diesel fuel. McVeigh drove it to the nine-story Alfred P Murrah Federal Building in Oklahoma City, Oklahoma because it had ATF, FBI and Drug Enforcement Agency federal employees in it. He had considered assassinating both Janet Reno and the sniper Lou Horiuchi who had been at Ruby Ridge and Waco, but decided on a truck bomb. He packed it in a big removal truck he hired. Wearing a T-shirt reading *Sic temper tyrrannis*, 'So it is always with tyrants', what Brutus said when he knifed Julius Caesar, he drove, lit time fuses, parked, got into his parked getaway car and drove off.

At 9.02 am 19 April 1995, the second anniversary of the Waco fire, it exploded. Local seismometers registered an earth tremor equivalent to 3 on the old Richter scale. Flying hunks of glass flying under tremendous pressure at terrific speeds was a big killer – glass fronted all storeys – but the collapse of the floors made crushing the major killer. The dead numbered 168, including 19 children; 680 were injured. An award-winning news shot of baby Baylee Almon in a fireman's arms became the symbol of the bombing; she died in hospital. The Oklahoma City bombing was, and remains, the deadliest act of domestic terrorism in US history.

About 10.30 am Oklahoma Highway Patrolman Charlie Hanger pulled a motorist over for driving a vehicle without number plates. The cop found illegal weapons in it and took, it turned out, Timothy McVeigh into custody, custody McVeigh would remain in until his trial, conviction, and death by lethal injection. Nichols got life without parole.

McVeigh in custody was allowed a voice, in an expression of democracy foreign to the repressive habits of Australian prison administrations, but natural to Americans. He was unrepentant and told it as he saw it. Federal agents acted like soldiers, so an attack on federal employees in a federal building was like an attack on a military command and control centre. McVeigh was asked about the children killed. He agreed 19 was a high 'for collateral damage' and if he had known there was a day-care place there, he might have chosen another target. This was greeted with howls of 'Bullshit!' People who knew the building and that McVeigh had scouted it out four months before, were adamant: no-one could miss the American Kids' Day Center, where 15 of the dead kids were.

The hated government responded by passing the Antiterrorism and Effective Death Penalty Act in 1996. The idea that the death penalty will deter murderers and terrorists, even ones like McVeigh who hoped to get away with it, has long been disproven. Such laws are aimed at the popular vote.

* * *

McVeigh was still alive in prison – he was not executed until 2011- during the Montana Standoff, the roots of which go way back.

An American who admired Adolf Hitler in the 1930s formed the Silver Shirts back then. He was an old retired dry cleaner in the 1960s, when Posse Comitatus (Force of the County), a far-right social movement for white Christians, was formed. Although defunct now, their beliefs and methods still have a major hold on the sovereign rights movement of the 2020s. Back in the 1960s they declared the county was the only legitimate form of government and the county sheriff the only lawman that counted; even then, if the sheriff did not obey the citizens, the Posse could at high noon hang the sheriff by the neck in a public spot, where he should remain dangling in the wind as an example to others until sundown.

The bits of government that they particularly did not believe in were the Inland Revenue Service, the federal taxation administrator; the Federal Reserve, who should have had gold reserves to back the phoney US dollar money but didn't; and almost anything with Jews, Satan's servants, thought to be in on it in some undefined way. In practical terms, they paid no taxes, ignored licensing but drove vehicles and owned guns, issued dud checks, and when bought to answer to courts they did not recognise as legitimate, perfected a kind of stonewalling they called 'paper terrorism'. They created ratbag documents of claim and counterclaim, mounted frivolous suits, argued the toss in semi-literate legal language at every chance they got, and sent their legal opponents and their judges spare. This is the Posse's bequest to the sovereign citizen movement who do it today. They could kill too. Gordon Kahl killed two US Marshals in North Dakota in 1983. But is the nature of far-right militant anti-government groups for their *names* to fade into oblivion.

The Montana Freemen were a far-right militant anti-government group who lived in Jordan, Montana (through they called it 'Justas Township'). In 2010 it had 343 citizens, 98.8 percent white; it was a few more in the mid-1990s but not many more. Not, I suspect, that anyone noticed at the time, but they declared themselves sovereign citizens along Posse Comitatus lines.

In March 1994 William Stanton, local rancher, was convicted of terrorism, 10 years in the can; he had used violence for political ends, so he fitted the terrorism bill. Next day, four men bearing arms calling themselves 'The Garfield County Four' tried to file papers in the court to stay the IRS's attempt to seize Rodney Skerddal's place. In 1995 foreclosure proceedings to take over the farmland Jordan/Justas stood on was irritating them. Locals held trials of their own, and issued a writ of execution on a named federal judge.

The FBI mounted an investigation into the mouthy locals' financial affairs and transactions. The locals, rather obviously, were easy pickings for FBI fraud investigators: a trail of dud cheque complaints, counterfeit cheques, tax evasion obvious from a total absence of returns, and so on. They arrested two men in March 1996 and issued arrest warrants for another eight.

The Montana Freemen armed up and confronted the FBI in a standoff. The FBI housed their tigers, memories of the Bureau's overreach on Ruby Ridge and at Waco still fresh, backed off, and tried negotiation. The man who had negotiated Randy Weaver's decision to turn himself in was hired. That man tried to bring Randy himself – over $3 million richer from government compensation and at a loose end for work – to come and talk with the Freemen. The FBI refused to allow the far-right's pin-up boy to get involved, but the Freemen knew their hero had tried.

But the negotiators gave up, meeting with nothing, they said, 'except religious and legal mumbo-jumbo'.[2] Other negotiators continued to talk to the Montana bores.

In mid-June 1996 negotiations ended after 81 days of jawing and trying not to yawn. The Montana Freeman Standoff was over and no blood was shed, not by the FBI, not by anyone else.

Mass killer Timothy McVeigh from custody claimed some credit for this first peaceful resolution between the FBI and 'patriots' like him. If the Oklahoma City bombing can be glossed over like this by its designer and perpetrator, as a leveller, what kind of mind are we dealing with?

After the 1990s but before the pandemic from effectively 2020, we must name a new way for far-right/alt-right online warriors to corral disagreeable information, especially information relayed by and presented on traditional media: it's 'fake news'. Total dismal.

But how do these guys – and some gals – deal with unkempt thoughts that creep into their heart or mind? Questions? Doubts? Disbelief? Conspiracy theorist's postings are characteristically unquestioning, certain and I'm-in-with-you, bro.

* * *

'Hello brother,' said a man at the door of the Al Noor Mosque during Friday prayers when a stranger approached. The stranger, helmeted with a GoPro webcam on it, wearing a flak jacket and emitting the music of military bands from a speaker hooked to it, was indeed strange. This stranger levelled a semi-automatic shotgun at him, and killed him. Then he fired shot through the door at those inside, switched to a semi-automatic Armalite rifle that fired bullets, and went into the prayer hall, killing and wounding wherever he went. Naseem Rashid, a Pakistani immigrant, charged at him but the gunman dropped him with a wound that proved fatal. Back outside, he killed another man, got another weapon from his car, and shot people there. Then he went back inside the prayer hall and blazed away at the wounded and anybody he saw and he had overlooked, before exiting, killing a woman outside, and driving off. He had other appointments to make.

The gunman parked aslant in the driveway of the Linwood Islamic Centre: no-one could get in or out by car. He couldn't find the door. No matter. He let rip through a window at the 100 or so people inside, then returned to his car. Abdul Aziz Wahabazada was outside, desperate for a weapon. Aziz seized on a card-reading scan-and-print payment machine and threw the puny thing at the gunman. A bit later, he picked up a discarded, unloaded shotgun, danced around shouting, 'I'm here.' When the gunman returned to his Subaru four-door saloon. Aziz threw the shotgun at him. The gunman drove off.

His plan was to drive to a town called Ashburton, 90 km south, and shoot up the Islamic 'invaders' there at another Friday prayer gathering.

The gunman had turned up at the Al Noor at 1.40pm. He exited Linwood at 1.55pm. Besides the obvious alarm bells going off, between the two kill sites, the gunman had taken Beasley Avenue in the city of

Christchurch, in the South Island of New Zealand. Beasley is a busy major civic thoroughfare. The gunman weaved, honked, used the median strip at speed, and was all over the shop.

The New Zealand Police had missed the gunman's car at the Al Noor. It was hidden by a bus, and as emergency cop mobile searches go, you can have thorough, or you can have speed, but you can't have both. These killings were *all* done in 15 minutes, six at the first mosque, less at the second. So, when the police vehicle found the erratically driven silver Subaru, they rammed the bastard's car hard. No one was going anywhere except the cop shop after that.

The murdering, 51 people were dead or would soon die, and the maiming of at least 40, not counting the wounded minds, was over.

The response of the nation of New Zealand, led by Prime Minister Jacinda Ardern and with her government united behind her, was as good as people, tribes or nations can do. New Zealanders' hearts went out to the orphans whose fathers and mothers had been senselessly shot dead or the parents mourning the death of a child. They were right behind their prime minister on this one. One decision she made was to never mention the perpetrator's name; the focus was to be, by her example, on the victims. And so it was, at the top.

This book does not have the luxury of choice. The gunman was Breton Harrison Tarrant, born 1990. Today, Melbourne neo-Nazis toast 'St Tarrant'. His manifesto of hate has been translated into Ukrainian, German, French and Russian.[3] He was a Grafton NSW boy who was living in Dunedin, 360 km south of Christchurch, when he planned out this crime.

His March 2019 crimes were dealt with by a New Zealand criminal court and he is to leave prison on his death, not before, an available sentence never before used. He wore the labels 'Islamophobic' and 'racist' in court. He denied being a nazi, but described himself as an 'eco- fascist', a far-right subordination of the individual to 'the land' or state blended with green politics, blaming overpopulation, immigration and overindustrialisation for environmental damage.

Grafton, the northern NSW city of 19 000 people where he grew up is noted for its jacaranda-lined streets and is no hotbed of far-rightism. The Tarrant family, teacher-mother, council-worker father, and two sons, Breton the younger, were respectable and respected, before and after the parents' split. Breton was close to his athletic father, who died young of mesothelioma and left a sizeable legacy to Breton, by then a 20-year-old personal trainer at a local gym. Judging by his Facebook posts back then he was looking for a 'goal… an ambition…'[4]

He travelled a good deal, almost always alone, and very widely: Europe, Asia, Africa… But one region stands out: the Balkans. The time he spent here was formative.

Tarrant drank in the heroic legends of the medieval and modern history of the clashes between Christian Europe and the Islamic Ottoman Empire and Türkiye. He never showed much interest in Christianity itself but saw the Christian Balkan tribes and nations as the white guys in the good-guy hats. He painted the names of some of their warrior heroes in the Cyrillic (or Slav) script used in the region on the weapons he used in Christchurch. Likewise, 'Remove Kebab'. 'Remove Kebab' is the name of a Serbian militaristic nationalist song of the 1990s, a time of war in the disintegrating Yugoslavia. The accordion player on the original recording spent seven years in a German prison for 14 murders committed in the wars; the song praises the Serb's 'ethnic cleansing' of Bosnian Muslims. It remains popular on far-right sites and memes. Tarrant also described himself as a 'kebab remover' in his scribblings. He played the tune as he drove up to the Al Noor Mosque's doors.

In Dunedin he led a loner's existence. He attended shoot meets at a rifle club and worked out in a gym. A gym worker there described him as a 'loner with a lot of money, but no job.'[5] Neighbours recall no visitors coming or going. Relatives from Australia who called in on him while holidaying saw no sign that he done much to make his flat a home. He did not appear to have put sheets on his bed, but he did fetch firearms from his car to show them. His mother became worried about his mental health.

On-line, and in the sick online world of 8Chan especially, he praised Anders Breivik; the Charleston church killer of nine, Dylann Storm Roof; and British Union of Fascists leader in the 1930s, Oswald Mosley. He called for the killings of German Chancellor Angela Merkel, Turkish President Recep Erdogan and London's mayor Sadiq Khan.

On the day of the killings, in a post that has an eerie similarity to Gareth Train's 'Rubicon' post, he sat in his car and typed, for 8Chan readers:

> Well lads, it's time to stop shitposting and time to make a real-life effort post. I will carry out and attack against the invaders, and will even live stream the attack via facebook.

There was a link to his Facebook home page and the manifesto full of words and symbols, including, for example, the Slavic-style swastikas, Odin's Cross and the resurrected 1930s German Nazi Black Sun symbol. The murdering swine was, like his online birds of a feather, extraordinarily fond of symbols. Even words, like the word 'Turkofagos' – Greek for *Turk-eater* – he used like a symbol, but this scrawl was in Latin script (just as he had written it on one of the firearms he carried). That and some mad drivel: was it a legacy statement? He must have known that at the end of the day, he would either be dead or on the way to a life in prison, a fate with only modest advantages over death.

Tarrant broadcast from the speaker on his flak jacket. When 'Remove Kebab' was done, the rousing fife-and-drum old stand- by 'The British Grenadier' would start up. He turned his head-cam-to-facebook gear on. And drove the short distance to the Al Noor Mosque.

* * *

This 2019 event was closer to home and an Australian citizen was its perpetrator. There are, at the time of writing, 29 listed terrorist organisations in the Australian federal criminal code – it's a crime to belong to, or to aid or abet them.

Most, 26, are Islamic extremist groups, mainly Sunni Islam ones like Boko Haram in West Africa to Indonesia's Jemmah Islamiyah in the east and many regions in between, listed from 2004 on.

Three are far-right white-supremacist ones. These were listed in 2021 or 2022.

The first, listed in August 2021, comes out of the UK: the Sonnenkrieg Division aka DKD Sun War Division. It is pro-Breivik, recommends raping female cops, and is against mixed-race sex. A DKD meme shows an image of Prince Harry about to be shot in the back of the head with 'See you later, race traitor' as caption.

Four months later, The Base made it there from North America. Its enemies are the current Jewish-controlled 'kike state' which must be destroyed by violent action, and it seeks to accelerate the, to them, inevitable 'race war'. They must win this to establish a 'white ethno-state'. They advocated lone-actor terrorist attacks and ran paramilitary training camps until 2020 when US law enforcement cracked enough of their cells to lay charges on many, and forced 'us [The Base] underground'.

In February 2022 the NSO, National Socialist Order aka Atomwaffen aka Atomic Weapons Division, got listed. This originally US organisation has cell members and leaders who also belong or used to belong to The Base cells. Except that the NSO has an occult addition – a secret Satanic Order of Nine Angles – it and The Base seem little more than a name change. The NSO are active recruiters through Telegram, Discord and Gab social media channels.

* * *

The Christchurch mosque-killer's Facebook video was swiftly archived by viewers before it was taken down. It has since been watched millions of times; in some quarters watched with sickening glee.[6] As we have seen, his long-winded manifesto circulates still.

Five months later 21-year-old Patrick Crusius drove from Dallas to the border town of El Paso and parked in a shopping centre carpark. He got out with a semiautomatic rifle and walked into the Walmart firing hollow-point bullets as he went, killing 23 and wounding 23 more. He then drove off to surrender to Texas Rangers nearby. He too had a manifesto, on 8chan:

> In general, I support the Christchurch shooter and his manifesto. This attack is a response to the Hispanic invasion of Texas. They are the instigators, not me. I am simply defending my country from cultural and ethnic replacement brought by an invasion… my motives … are not at all personal. Actually the Hispanic community was not my target before I read The Great Replacement.

A week or so passed. Norwegian Phillip Manshaus had been reading the Christchurch shooter's manifesto too. The 21 year-old posted his admiration for its author and his intention to kill on a message board:

> Well cobbers it's my time, I was elected by saint Tarrant after all. We can't let this go on, you gotta bump the race war thread irl [in real life] and if you're reading this you have been elected by me… [Valhalla awaits].

He could not get his livestream gear to work, or it was swiftly removed – reports vary. Then he went into the bedroom of his sleeping 17 year-old stepsister and shot her dead. She had been adopted into the family at 2 years old in China. Then he drove to the Al Noor Islamic Centre and shot the lock off the mosque door. Inside, the three men there overpowered and disarmed him, and he was in a choke hold when police arrived. Manshaus was sentenced to 21 years, renewable if he is still considered a threat in 2040.

Two months passed. A 27 year-old neo-nazi Stephan Balliet switched his livestream cam on and tried to enter a synagogue in Halle, Germany and kill Jews to weaken the power of the so-called Zionist Occupation Government. 'If every white man kills just one, we win.' He could not get in, and shot a woman dead on the street outside and then drove to a Turkish kebab shop and shot it up. A customer died, and he wounded two other victims. Police in force penned his car in, and arrested him. Balliet was sentenced to life in prison.

What sustains these men as they endure the dreary sameness of days in the can, the tiny world of prison life?

I think the answer to that question is the same thing that put them in there: a belief that they can see the future.

When journalists Nick McKenzie and Joel Tozer had a plant inside Tom Sewell's Victorian neo-nazi group at what the group called 'Racism HQ' meetings, he recorded a member saying of the race war they believe is to come, 'It is coming, dude. It's not a matter of if, it's when'. And of 'St Tarrant' in his New Zealand can, Sewell says with conviction, 'He'll be in there until we win the revolution. Like Nelson Mandela. He's got until we win. He doesn't come out until then. So, exactly, he's putting us on a timeline.'[7]

QAnon adherents await The Great Awakening too. Others prophecy the Fall of the Cabal. Or the Race War.

The future that the Trains saw was the apocalypse before The Rapture and Second Coming, though enduring prison life was not in their plan. Their plan seemed to involve rising from the dead.

History is full of failed prophecies, but blind faith goes on and on.

* * *

At a memorial service in Chinchilla for Matthew and Rachel that Keely Brough attended, there was a man who knew pain and loss by the hand of a cop killer, Luke Forte. His brother Brett (Fortie) Forte had once been a cop stationed there.

But Senior Constable Brett Forte was with the Toowoomba Tactical Crime Squad when, aged 57, married to Susan (Susie) Forte, a cop herself, with three children, when he was fatally shot one night in May 2017.

His fatal journey started after an arrest warrant was issued. Domestic Violence Prevention unit cops were contacted by a woman who had had petrol poured over her and been threatened with a clearly working 'pirate' handgun by her partner, a big hulking muscular man given to wild mood swings, particularly when drinking, one with an extensive criminal history, a hatred of police and a fondness for guns: Ricky Maddison. One of the DV unit cops who counselled the fearful complaint was Senior Constable Susan Forte.

Maddison went on the run for a couple of months, using payphones to contact police and his ex-partner and, given to paranoia, felt Susan and Brett (who was active in tracking him) had it in for him. Brett had taken a call from him, which he handed over to another officer. He drove to spot near a public phone booth. The Tactical Squad had sighted a Nissan vehicle associated with Maddison just before 2 pm in suburban Toowoomba. Maddison was confirmed to be its driver.

Three marked police vehicles fell in behind Maddison, SC Brett Forte driving TW208 with SC Catherine Nielsen in the passenger seat being the leader of the, at first, relatively sedate suburban pursuit, Maddison obeying speed limits and road rules.

Then Maddison suddenly left the highway in the Lockyer Valley, off-road. He turned into Wallers Road, a single-lane dirt dead-end. 'It's like he's leading us somewhere,' Forte said. Nielsen said, 'I just thought the exact same thing.'

At the brow of a rise, at 2.18 pm, Maddison slowed to a stop, and he got out with a rifle. He had led the three pursuit vehicles into ambush.

TW208's dashcam recorded Brett: '... automatic gunfire, automatic gunfire, urgent, automatic gunfire'. Silent on that record but visible, were the holes in the windscreen. Maddison emptied a magazine, reloaded and emptied that too. Over 40 rounds were fired, over 20 hit TW208, six entered the cabin, one hit Brett's arm, another his groin. Catherine Nielsen radioed: '... we're sitting ducks... [he's] 50 metres away...' (Later, she would say, 'It was one after another, after another, after another. It was something like from the streets of Beirut.')

Brett locked into R and reversed in order to put some more distance between them and the gunman. He rolled TW208, perhaps making a turn, perhaps simply losing control or consciousness, and it stopped belly up at the bottom of the road embankment, bullets still hitting it. He probably saved Catherine's life in this last act. No bullet had hit her.

She reported 'Fortie's in a bad way. There's blood. We need a hand here.' She smashed the windscreen under fire. Doors jammed shut, she opened a way to get him out. One of the other pursuit car's occupants ditched plans to don bullet-proof gear, just went straight to TW208 and their colleagues. Brett Forte died there unconscious of loss of blood. His wife Susie had followed events on the police radio. Queensland Police much later released TW208's chilling car cam video from picking up the tail to spinning in the embankment.

Maddison knew where he was going, a bushland hidey-hole he and friends used for drinking and shooting with an illegal modified SKS semi-automatic rifle, a Soviet military weapon. The weapon he used to kill or try to kill, to him at the time, anonymous police on his tail was an illegal US-made Kris Corp KS30. Thousands of rounds were stored there. He was at the gate to it when he opened fire on TW208.

SERT and Polair were soon all over it. A siege followed into the night.

Maddison communicated with SERT negotiators, feeling sorry for himself, saying he was shocked that a man had died at his hand, expressing sympathy for the family, being smartarsed, making outlandish requests for individuals to be brought to him, discharging rounds at a helicopter and an armoured vehicle, and refusing to put him hands up and walk out.

He got angry when his vehicle was disabled at daylight and grew increasingly fatigued, erratic and paranoid. After 20 hours of standoff, around 11 am next day, he rushed a cop who shot him dead.

There was an inquest six years later. Many felt that was an unconscionably long wait. State Coroner Terry Ryan concluded it on 14 March 2023. He essentially found that reports to police of automatic gunfire at the Wallers Road property had been incorrectly attributed to a licensed shooter, and that the information had not been uploaded to QPRIME, the police database, but was entered into the wrong system; thus the Tactical Squad were not alerted to Maddison's potential to be armed. He also ruled that SCs Susan Forte and Nielsen should not have been subject to an internal investigation.[8]

Susie Forte and Catherine Nielsen were critical of police information sharing. They said police had been told Maddison had automatic weapons at the bush hidey-hole and had talked about 'taking out' police, told to them by the concerned father of an addict. His son and some drug dealers there had seen the weapons, heard the words. If, SC Nielsen said, that information had been shared with her and SC Forte, pursuit would not have been considered. Not an option; a tactic not on. But it had not been. Therefore, QPS had a problem. SC Susan Forte agreed. And she further said the QPS was doing a 'cover up' job.

Office politics in police is tough, from the area station's locker room to HQ. Both women reported senior officers were dismissive of their questions, bullied them, and used a follow-this-line-or-else attitude. Catherine said they made her 'life hell', her workplace 'toxic'; Susie recalled colleagues asking, 'Are you trying to get police into trouble?' and telling her she risked looking like a 'vindictive widow'.

Susan lawyered up for the Forte-Maddison inquest. She felt she was being thwarted on the stand. But as a widow she had a right to read and file a Victim Impact Report at the end of proceedings. Hers was a 9000-word one. Clearly, she had included conclusions of her private investigation, research, records of interactions, and of course, how Brett's death impacted on her and the kids. Her barrister's request to have her read it in court and hand it up as an exhibit on the record was opposed by the QPS's barrister, who said there was a lot wrong with it, but particularly that it was 'defamatory'.

Brother-in-law Luke rode shotgun for her throughout. He made public statements she, a police officer, could not make. And he made the journey to the Chinchilla cop shop to offer his unique condolences.

* * *

Between Fortie's death and the Wieambilla shootings, no Queensland police officer was fatally shot. In the early hours of a night in June 2021 53-year-old SC David Masters was laying road spikes to deflate the tires of a stolen car and intercept the occupants. The car hit and killed him, and kept going. Two women were later charged, case yet to be concluded.

1 Jason Wilson, *Guardian* 26 August 2017

2 'Bo Gritz abandons negotiations with the Montana Freeman', *South Coast Today*, 2 May 1996

3 Kristy Milligan, 'Australia's Right-wing landscape: local threats in transnational context', *Periscope*, November 2012

4 Tim Brown, 'A loner with a lot of money', Radio New Zealand, 24 August 2020

5 Tim Brown, 'A loner with a lot of money', Radio New Zealand, 24 August 2020

6 Kristy Campion, *Chasing Shadows: the untold and deadly story of terrorism in Australia*, 2022

7 'Inside Racism HQ: how home-grown neo-nazis are plotting a white revolution', *Age* 16 August 2021

8 Alexandria Utting, '"Several systemic factors" may have contributed to fatal shooting of Queensland police officer Brett Forte by Ricky Maddison, coroner finds', ABC News, 14 March 2023

11
Gareth Train's Uploads

I am a son of Yahweh the creator God…
Yeshua is my king and brother.
– Gareth Train on an online forum. Yeshau: *Hebrew,* Jesus

Gareth Daniel Train filled some of his time, mornings especially, when Stacey was still teaching in Tara, reading and commenting on blogs. As my mother used to say, 'The devil makes work for idle hands.'

Nathaniel and Stacey's daughter Madelyn or Maddy, charted by phone and email how stepfather Gareth, Gary to her, struggled to find work and as a result spent more and more time online, plunging him deeper and deeper into conspiracy theories, she said.

'I know he spent a lot of time on the internet. You watch one weird video on YouTube and then the algorithm sends you on a weird fucking Alice-in-Wonderland trip where you're watching heaps of weird shit. And that's all it feeds you… He would send me links to shit and I'd go, that's a bit weird. He would send me YouTube stuff – like, repeatedly, send me weird links. I didn't even really look. I knew I had read enough to say "That's weird" to Gary and Gary just wouldn't say anything. They just contacted me too much about shit that I didn't want to hear about, like Covid shit that I thought was not accurate. It was not like, "Hi, how are you?" It was like, "Here's this Covid conspiracy theory – BOOM!"'

Did Gareth hope to recruit Maddy to his cause? Stacey, on her last day, dropped into conspiracist-to-conspiracist video upload, her view of that. She clearly considered her children to be lost, weirdly heretical for not buying into, perhaps signing up to the parental Trains' awful one true path.

'They were always spiritually minded,' said Maddy. 'And they believed literally that Covid was the end of the world.' Boarding school life and a working life, last job with a health and safety company in the Far North had immunised her and presumably Aidan against 'weird shit'.[1]

* * *

The earliest online comment of Gareth's I have found is from November 2020, two years before the killings.[2]

Martyn Bryant, he opined, was 'the perfect patsy' to blind us to the truth that the Port Arthur Massacre was 'a Government Psychological Operation to disarm the Australian population' with the 'CIA, MI6, Mossad, ASIO and the Australian SASR [Special Air Service Regiment]' working behind the scenes. In another comment on that massacre, he blamed 'MK shooters' for those killings and woundings, and that the SAS killed the shooters in turn to keep the whole thing secret. MK Ultra was the codename for a real top-secret, illegal CIA research and experimental program using covert LSD drugging, mind control, brainwashing, etc of human subjects. The program was bought to an end by media exposure by the *New York Times* and the Rockefeller Commission in the 1970s.

Obviously, the eyewitnesses who saw Bryant do it, the Tasmanian cops and the harlots of the press had all been duped, but Gareth on his block knew. He saw false flag operations everywhere, and one morning in June the next year he wised up anyone reading and listed a few of them [words in brackets added]:

Cleaning house

David Opas [Family Law Court judge, murder victim]
Colin Winchester [ACT assistant police commissioner, murder victim]
Victor Chang [cardiac surgeon, murder victim]
John Newman [NSW politician, murder victim]
Manipulated collective memory
1984 'Bombing' of the Parramatta Family Law Court
1987 'Queen Street massacre', Frank Vitkovic
1990 'Surry Hills massacre', David Anthony Evers
1991 'Strathfield massacre', Wade Frankum
1997 'Backpacker murders 80s – 92, Ivan Milat
1994 NCA [National Crime Authority, Adelaide] bombing
The program's false flags never stopped

Also in 2020 Gareth pitched a conspiracy theory nearly as stupid as QAnon :

> Military invention (martial law storm troopers) is the aim. I have said it before but I'll say it again. Australian politics is a bicephalic serpent and US politics not any different although it may be an ouroboros [an ancient Egyptian symbol, serpent swallowing its tail]. The cabal controls ALL. Politics is interactive entertainment to keep the brain-dead masses distracted. [Punctuation here and below is very slightly changed here for clarity.]

In September that year, when Covid-19 infections were raging and government restrictions announced, he suggested he had been a conspiracy theorist for a long time. He had, he wrote, 'been trying reach people as individuals for the past 25 years and convince them of the WWO [?], UN, WHO [World Health Organisation], Reset [an economic recovery from coronavirus plan, but a socialist plot here], 1%er's [the richest percentile, but a capitalist plot here] plans and the use of silent weapons for quiet wars.'

On a private forum Gareth wrote of missing out on formal education 'due to [his] critical evaluations of teaching practices and resulting conflicts.' He wrote of his experience of university as a mature-age student studying social work: 'In doing so I discovered the religions of education and psychology... I soon learned their high priests were the same indoctrinating snakes as the church high priests.'

On 12 January 2021 Deborah commented that something or other, possibly an encryption program or a secure communication channel, 'was safe. Wikileaks recommend it…' Gareth weighed in on Deborah's naivety:

> Wikileaks is playing their part in the muppet show. Does Wikileaks know they are playing they are playing a part? They f@cking should by now.
>
> QAnon , Q Psy Op – open your eyes and return to reality.
>
> Question everything.

'Reality' is a much-abused word when conspiracy idiots write and speak. They reveal an extraordinary contempt for evidence, blind faith in themselves and their simplistic view of the world, use breath-taking planet-wide generalisations, adopt utter certainty in their tone, and, in responding, seize on a word or phrase to launch their tangent. The contemptuous egotistical use of Deborah's 'Wikileaks' is used as the hook to say, *You wouldn't know shit, girlie.* Also, Gareth is sloppy. Does he mean QAnon is part of 'they'? Or just another of those Psy Ops? My major source, who wades in these sewers a lot more than I am willing to do, thinks Gareth dismisses QAnon here. Gareth's idea of a 'Question' leaves out doubt. He has all the answers.

About an hour later, same blog spot, he posted a quotation from Joseph Plumb, Connecticut Yankee veteran of the American War of Independence who wrote a book. The passage is about those who ran away when the shooting started; they are cowards who do not therefore 'share the glory or earn a place in the life of our Republic'.

In the next month there was a lockdown protest in Melbourne where things got ugly, police got tear gas out, and the protest hit the blogosphere. Gareth was sceptical:

> What is the theatre of organised protest really about? What is really accomplished? Why do so many people insist on peaceful demonstrations while being assaulted and taken prisoner by corporate soldiers aka police? Why do protestors stand by and film their compatriots, family and friends mistreated and humiliated? Why do protesters run away from a fight they will have to have at some point?

What will you choose when the wolf is at your door?

And:

> There is no political or legal way out of what is upon us. It is down to the individual and the choices they make in everything they do going forward. Be aware of those who promise a political or legal way out only offering distraction, while enslaving you through false hope.

We leave Gareth Train here, 11 months away from murder.

* * *

Freelance journalist and analyst Elise Thomas concluded Gareth Train did not subscribe to 'a single conspiracy theory [but]... a multitude of conspiracy theories and to have interpreted almost everything in the context of these theories. Conspiracy theories referenced in his comments include anti-vaccine and anti-lockdown narratives, climate engineering and Sovereign Citizen conspiracies, conspiracies about microchips, the New World Order and Great Reset, the Illuminati, antisemitic conspiracy theories and more. Gun control conspiracy theories... feature heavily...'[3] The New World Order refers to geo-political shifts which will follow the pandemic; the Great Reset refers to the plan of the World Economic Forum for recovery from the pandemic hatched in Davos Switzerland in June 2020. Gareth called Covid-19 shots 'neurological bio-weapons'.

Gareth's taste for doomsday prepping and Sovereign Citizen ideas are apparent from signpost usage of '*ark*, *homesteading*, *preparing* and *survive*' in this web post:

> I currently live on my rural property in western Queensland where I have been building an 'ark', homesteading for the last five years preparing to survive tomorrow. I am not interested in indoctrinating or convincing anyone of anything.

When Gareth dismisses political action as useless, Elise Thomas makes the point that this is a common sentiment in the on-line footprints of 'mass shooters and other perpetrators of extremist violence'.

Her analysis did not throw up a religious strand as Queensland Police and ASIO analysts later saw, in Religiously Motivated Violent Extremism as prime mover. They have, of course, more material and the words of Nathaniel and Stacey Train as well. But premillennialism, Christianity and the divine is absent in Gareth's web posts, except for the use of the word 'Christian' in this raving off-the-cuff list:

> If you are a conservative, anti-vaxx, freedom lover, protester, common law, conspiracy talker, alternative news, independent critical thinker, truther [9/11 truth movement, '9/11 was an inside job'], Christian, patriot etc etc expect a visit from these hammers — they are here to kill, maim and take you to re-education school.

His anti-police sentiments are plain, a central obession.

* * *

In May 2022 Gareth set up an account with YouTube he called @mrsyugirawil, YouTube handle 'Mrs Yugi girawil'. But he uploaded no videos until November. The account's table-of-contents dashboard in the period immediately after the shootings had 12 videos uploaded, about 36 minutes viewing in total, six subscribers, and garnered viewers in the low tens, except for the last, with over 200. Gareth had sent his ravings into the ether where they were largely ignored. But the last was sent under siege and not taken down until after the harlots of the mainstream media were all over the vileness in Wieambilla.

This author subscribes to *Crikey!* Their journo Cam Wilson found 'Mrs girawil' and wrote an old-fashioned scoop which I found in my Inbox 16 December 2022. Guessing police, alerted by Wilson's story, would ask Youtube to remove it, I immediately watched all the videos, some more than once, the last one a lot, in great haste before all disappeared: it was taken down that day.

The following is from my scribbled notes. The order of Gareth's uploads is algorithmically programmed and followed here. After the last few uploaded, where time of day and absolute dates are clear, the dates are as close as YouTube's, say, 'three weeks ago' allows.

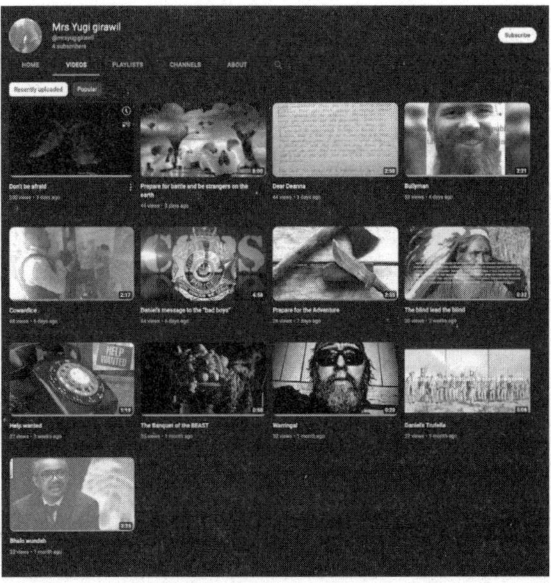

Image: Youtube/Mrs Yugi Girawil

Gareth appears to have also uploaded on an account with Rumble, a site with greater tolerance for conspiracy theories, bigotry and contemptuous language than Youtube.

* * *

From early to 26 November 2022, the first three Youtube videos were uploaded:

Daniel's Truefella

Gareth online usually referred to himself in the third person, as 'Daniel', his middle name. 5:06 minutes. Historical photos of First Australian people, some shackled, many of them children in church and state educational institutions. The audio was the Warumpi Band's call to racial harmony, 'Blackfella/whitefella':

> Blackfella, whitefella, yellafella, anyfella
> It doesn't matter what your color
> As long as you a true fella

Overscript: 'church and state enslave the mind'.

Warrigal

Gareth wearing sunglasses speaking on web cam for 20 seconds, voice heavily distorted and largely inaudible.

('Warrigal' is an Aboriginal name for a *feral, wild* dingo, horse or weed; also, for *to hear.*)

The Banquet of the BEAST

Lush food shots with a female voice thought to be Stacey's intoning a sermon verse rap for 58 seconds.

Between 21 and 27 November, two more were published and viewed less than 30 times:

Help wanted

Opens showing (as its thumbnail image above) a vintage cradle desk phone. 1:19 minute long. Other content features a cartoon mouse. Its message is not clear beyond perhaps a call to arms – the help wanted?

The blind lead the blind

The latter's thumbnail is what appears to be a portrait of an American Indian chief with an illegible quotation, is a 32-second one.

* * *

The five November videos above are relatively innocuous compared to what's to come, and show a security consciousness. December's seven videos below are all ominous, threatening and drip with violent intent, and the creator is more careless about details that identify them. The first was uploaded four days before they killed, the second, three days and so on.

Prepare for the Adventure

A single black-and-white photo image of a hatchet, knife and what looks like a whetstone for sharpening them, is on screen over the whole 2:55 min. Voiceovers: 'love and obey your heavenly father', and the opening of Psalm 46 'God is our refuge and strength, a very present help in trouble'. Music: the 1960s Ben E King spiritual-inspired but made love song – delivered to 'darling' – long a classic, 'Stand by Me':

> No, I won't be afraid,
> No, I won't be afraid
> Just as long as you
> Stand by me

(The juxtaposition of grim graphics with the sweetly seductive music, the positivity implied by the title, and the God-is-on-on-our-side voiceovers, have elements of the general's morale-boosting address to the troops before battle. Is it addressed to Stacey and/or Nathaniel? This was uploaded on 8 December; the day NSW Police published the missing person report.)

Daniel's message to the 'bad boys'

Dated 10 December, two days out from murder, Daniel – Gareth – opens with *Cops* TV show screen titling and theme song 'Bad Boys', performed by Jamaican reggae artists, Inside Circle:

> Bad boys, whatcha want
> Watcha want, whatcha gonna do?
> When sheriff John Brown come for you
> Tell me whatcha wanna do, whatcha gonna do?
> [Chorus]
> Bad boys, bad boys
> Whatcha gonna do?
> Whatcha gonna do when they come for you?

It ends with an image of an axe and knife, Gareth saying, 'You wish to make this public by using my little bother?'

Gareth's heavily disguised voice, sounding like a Dalek in *Dr Who*, intones 'Here's a message for following people.' He lists police officers who he names with rank and phone extension numbers, three with Queensland Police and one, dubbed 'Inspector Gadget', with NSW Police. State police badges shown as appropriate. 'Pay attention. Let's get straight to the question that all you boys want answered. I don't know why you all were born retarded enough to join the police force. I guess it is to do with your mother [*inaudible* domestic? enough dick?]. Possibly. But you all made the choice.'

He then mentions, as an example of how retarded police are, how the

Queensland Police failed to find a Sergeant Baker, who was on the run from them 'for two years'.

This no doubt referred to ex-Senior Sergeant Daniel Baker of the two-person station in Camooweal where Gareth and Stacey lived in 2011 and 2012. Depressed, in the maw of gambling and alcohol addictions, the sergeant did not make cash deposits for the Department of Transport and Main Roads and other government bodies when the station acted as their agent in the tiny town and people came in to pay cash for licences and the like for two years. He used the cash to repay personal loans and he intended to pay it all back when he was dealt that card so high and wild he'd never have to deal another. That card wasn't dealt him in 2015 or in 2016 or before March 2017 when he resigned. Inevitably, 'But-I-paid-it…' complaints led to investigators finding he had misappropriated $18,000 or so, and saw a warrant put out for him to appear in the Mt Isa Magistrates' Court. He did not front. He was arrested in Darwin in February 2019, extradited, and went down on six fraud, theft and misconduct charges, imprisoned for three-and-a-half years.

Daniel: 'Talk with Sergeant Baker ex-QPS retard [and ask] him what happens when you come up on old Daniel here, and pull your pistols.' Nothing is known about any personal or police interaction between SS Baker and Gareth Train, but complaints to police about Gareth's behaviour were made.

The named cops included one from the CPIU – 'Child Protection Investigation Unit, for our American friends' – with whom he said he had acrimonious dealings. (Proceedings in the Family Court, where child-protection issues are dealt with, are *never* reported. This silence is legislated. Therefore, Gareth's obvious beef with the police unit that deals with such matters is, and may remain, effectively a state secret. This contact with the CPIU might relate to Stacey and Nathaniel's children, and to Stacey and Gareth's care of them. Or perhaps to one of the many

Camooweal State School parent's complaints at how Gareth behaved. It could relate to his brief stint with the CPIU in 2009 as he added 'That's right. Ol' Daniel been around the block a few times.'

'I suggest you boys that drive all the way out here and stand around at my front gate having a circle jerk, trying to find your testicles, just put an end to that shit.'

The threatening tone makes this post ominous.

He introduces an animated cartoon 'Once upon a time there were three little birds…' The cartoon is of a mouse-in-need sleeping in a jar of mousseline taking a call on a bedside phone from an unseen cheese shop proprietor offering cheddar, blue Stilton and Cornish yarg. The mouse hangs up, eats cheese that came through the phoneline gratis and goes up in flame. Of the 4 minutes 23 seconds posted, a quarter is devoted to this mouse yarn, its message, if any, obscure.

Cowardice

Uploaded 10 December 2022, this showed four-day-old hand-cam footage of New Zealand police officers taking 'Baby W', who doctors testified would die without cardiac surgery, from a domestic situation, from its strenuously objecting anti-vaxx parents, after a court order was made. This order over-ruled the parent's objections to the child receiving 'vaccinated' blood by transfusion in theatre.

Gareth: For 200 years here in Australia and New Zealand, you have allowed your masters and their agents to do as they will to the children… There is no point making placards and protesting. Either defend children to their last breath or answer for cowardice.

MK Ultra gets a mention again. So too does ASIO's Mike Burgess, for his recently published threat assessment on pandemic-related radical extremism.

(Baby W had the surgery, anti-vaxx demonstrators outside the hospital, and survived. Gareth presumably thought the parents should have physically resisted the cops, ambos and medics – hence they are cowards, as the thumbnail's title dubs it.) 2:17 min.

Bullyman

Uploaded Sunday, 11 December, murders' eve. Nathaniel does not speak or appear on camera in any of Mrs Yugi girawli's videos but his portrait – a still close-up photo of full-bearded Nathaniel – shows throughout this video, the photo provided to NSW Police and used by them in publicising the missing-person. And Nathaniel is the subject of this 2:21-minute video. Gareth, robot-voiced, reads out the missing person report, and says, 'I see there was no mention of this missing person being a whistle-blower on high level corruption within the New South Wales education department' and 'connections to the NSW Police organised crime syndicate and fixated persons branch'. He uses, what are in retrospect, ominous words about missing person reports and 'so-called welfare checks.' While 'Daniel' does not date the actual day, the welfare check call at Wains Road is clearly expected there, and soon.

* * *

Monday, 12 December turned out to be the day the Trains killed. Three videos were uploaded that day.

Dear Deanna

Posted early that day, Stacey, as 'Jane,' her middle name, reads for 2:50 minutes a letter she has handwritten (a still of which forms the background image) to Deanna, an online Christian fellow traveller she's found. Jane warns Deanna that Deanna must leave where she is. In what seems like a reference to a previous sharing of motherly problems, Jane laments: 'I know the pain of losing children. Recently my husband and I lost both our adult children when they choose the world, rejecting us to take their wide road that their partners and friends are on. This is a pain that will only be healed in heaven.' She recommends Deanna contact 'Don' of Arizona, another fellow traveller.

(Is this tidying up of her online social affairs Stacey's suicide note? Preparing to stand by – and die beside – her man?)

Prepare for battle and be strangers on the earth

Posted 1.41pm. At 8 minutes, a record length for this account. The thumbnail pic is pink-lit rows of jawless human skulls on shelves, more inside. Lightning patterns, black background, and other apocalyptic graphics. Female voice – Stacey's? – intoning a mad sermon with a very scary god: 'War looms, sinners will be punished on judgement day.'

There is quotation from 2 Esdras. This was originally written, in Aramaic, by an unknown Jew called Ezra – a fifth-century scribe perhaps – at a bad time for Jewish aspirations: the Romans occupied Jerusalem. The writings were revealed to an influential, presumably Christian, seer and became a book of the New Testament. It is an obscure book: in English bibles it is usually left out or consigned to an appendix. Perhaps only those such as the sons of a New Testament scholar, as the Train brothers were, would know of it, although apocalyptic futures can, apparently, also be found by the determined in Matthew, Mark, Luke and John too. The thrust of 2 Esdras is unremittently apocalyptic, that the present age of much evil will be replaced with a future heavenly age when the righteous few will survive the final judgement and live forever after. Quoted is 2 Esdras 28: 'For of a city there shall be 10 left, and two of the field, which shall hide themselves in the thick groves, and in the clefts of the rocks,' Or premillennialism, which Queensland Police have called out as the root cause of this horror.

In YouTube comments, an accountholder, Gareth using 'Daniel' in the third person, adds: 'After dealing with covert agents and tactics for some time now, Daniel believes that should they choose to cross the Rubicon with public state actors, our Father is giving us a clear sign. Monsters and their heads are soon parted.' And 'You attempt to abduct us using contractors. You attempt to intimidate and target us with your Raytheon Learjets and planes. You send covert assets out here to my place in the bush… What is your play here? To have me and my wife murdered during a state police "welfare check"? You already tried that one… eat shit and die.'

In retrospect 'Prepare for battle …' seems hideously apt though 'battle' is pitched overly heroically for the ambush and cold-blooded killing of unsuspecting victims. Cam Wilson muses 'hide themselves in the thick groves, and in the clefts of the rocks' may be a reference to the camouflage clothing they wore while lying in ambush on 12 December; if so, Con Keely Brough in police blues, a fit ex-personal trainer, thankfully proved better at it. The Rubicon – the point where there is no going back- will be the homestead's fence; of course. This Rubicon is only known to the gunners; to the cops, it is just a fence. 'Our Father' has blessed the intended killings, given them divine right to kill. The cops are 'monsters', 'public sate actors', 'covert assets' perhaps – though they could be expected to be, and were, in uniform – and hell-bent on murdering the Trains, self-appointed victims. How could Gareth convince himself, his wife and brother that a routine call by police – the worst rational foreseeable result of which would see Nathaniel fined for covid border-busting and firearms offences – as attempts to murder them? Stacey was dominated by Gareth and had been isolated on the block with him for a year. Nathaniel had lived for 16 months since his heart attack and resultant mental impairment, though his state of mind in the last half of 2022 is not known. I believe this video is proof enough that the trio had made a suicide pact.

Don't be afraid

This last YouTube video was uploaded at 7.39 pm, around three hours after cutting down Rachael and Matthew. Alan too is dead, and the Trains are besieged. Helicopter surveillance is well established. Outside, SERT had taken over the siege from the Western Downs cops.

Gareth and Stacey on webcam are in a room lit only by the computer screen, in the underground bunker perhaps. Gareth: 'They came to kill us and we killed them. If you don't defend yourself against these devils and demons, you're a coward.' Stacey, to Don: 'We'll see you when we get home, Don. Love you' Gareth echoed this farewell.

Two hours before this final post, a comment addressed to Don, an American Youtuber given to commenting on their videos, went out from the killers in the third person: THEY'VE CROSSED THE RUBICON.

'Home' is the afterlife. This post is uninformative about the details of what they have just done, created before the events became public and designed to be read after that. For two people who know they are about to die, they affect being reconciled to it; no regrets here. For people who have just taken human lives, they are unphased, even perhaps smug, about it. They have again reduced human beings they did not know to abstractions, but this time to quasi-religious moral abstractions embodying evil: 'demons and devils'. They are sober in manner, but there is no remorse, no regret. Everything is due to the actions of the unmentioned police and the 'state'. For their part, the yoke of necessity was placed on their necks and honour compelled them to 'defend' themselves.

* * *

I do not pretend to understand the thinking that led the Trains to shoot people dead and to die by gun as they did, but they clearly invited this awful, bloody last day, bought on their own End of Days and thus in an earthly sense, fulfilled their bizarre prophecies.

I do not know when they resolved to set this into action either. The December posts show they were ready to kill five days out from when the four police officers turned up, but I suspect their private resolution, their kill-and-death-pact was made well before that. Two of the trio were asking for camouflage clothing in Western Downs shops two months before, well before the missing person report was published, for example.[4]

Why? Why is an impossible question to answer. Their twisted theology, undisciplined pseudo-logical and illogical connections, and mad-as-cactus politics defeat the usual tools I bring to analyse cause and motivation. For instance, Peter Morrall's Four Ls for murder– lust (kill rival), love (mercy killing of a loved one), loathing and loot – are of no help at all.[5]

Aside from war crimes, organised crime organisations' hits, gang wars and the like – violent, homicidal but understandable – three killers acting in homicidal concert is rare. The *folie à trois* murder, where three people come to share a psychosis is especially rare. (The classic *folie à deux* is the Parker-Hulme case, dramatized in the film *Heavenly Creatures;* two schoolgirls kill the mother of one of them to avoid their separation by a planned move abroad.) As psychosis is essentially a state of delusion, the reader will see my temptation here. The DSM-5 has the old *folie à deux, trois* and *quatre* on the newish schizophrenic spectrum and in other personality disorders. One dominant deluded soul can induce the delusion in others if the others are receptive types: nature's submissives, the taught-to-be worn-down, the coerced, the buffeted unanchored looking for a safe harbor, the gullible… Could Gareth, who took over the girl here and got the affection of at least one of her and Nathaniel's kids; who was the 'control-freak' in Camooweal Stacey was reported to be totally in thrall to; the perpetrator of a witnessed act of physical violence on her there; and who spent her last year on the 251 Wains Road block pretty well 24/7 with just him and, for some unknown times, his brother, her ex- and a damaged man who she had nursed and made decisions for. Nathaniel had from childhood played second fiddle to his older brother, and the heart attack 16 months before may have robbed him of a wish to, or the ability to resist. One psychological objection to this *folie à trois* idea is Gareth's diagnosis of Autism Spectrum Disorder, which does not conform with it. Auties may well demonstrate leadership abilities, but they do not create heartless fanatics among those who report to her or him.

Nevertheless, while all three were enthusiastic shooters, executioners, and hunters in the grass until SERT bullets killed them, Gareth is the only contender for being the driving force of this mindless bloodletting. He is, in my view, primarily responsible for the death of five people and his own on that awful day in Wieambilla.

1 Kevin Airs, 'Cop killers' paedophile "secret": How evil preppers' spiral into doomsday conspiracies started with a rift within the family over child abuse allegations,' *Daily Mail Australia* 30 January 2023

2 Elise Thomas, 'Wieambilla shooting: analysis of perpetrators' online footprint', Institute for Strategic Dialogue, no date

3 Ditto

4 7News with APP, 19 December 2022

5 *Murder and Society: why commit murder?* Centre for Crime & Justice Studies, 2007

12
The Response

Anarchism is a game at which the police can beat you.
– George Bernard Shaw

In Chapter 1 we left Western Downs police officers scrambling to get to 251 Wains Road to do whatever they could to help colleagues there, and Brisbane police headquarters getting Pol Air in the air over the scene and a Special Emergency Response Team on the road to the shooters' grounds.

The Queensland Police Service have lowered a curtain on what happened next. This is entirely reasonable management for an organisation which must investigate evidence coolly – ensure the crime scene is safe to work in; reconstruct timelines; seal and search the scene; get reports from witnesses, pathologists, ballistics, IT experts and others; chase down rumours; and much else – and look at the big picture, at least until the service is ready to present it to the coroner's court.

The Homicide Group will oversee the investigation and do most of the work. The involvement of Ethical Standards Command is automatic whenever a police officer kills someone, anyone, however justifiable, as here, that homicide appears to be. ESC had taken 152 statements by June 2023, and the brief for the corner had a way to go before it was ready. Liaison with NSW Police will be necessary, as the originators of the Missing Person report and what Nathaniel did on their side of the border on what looks like a small-time gun-running exercise and fiasco. There may have been a phone request from NSW Police direct to Chinchilla Police Station.

The curtain QPS lowered has been petty effective. But admiration has a way of lifting curtains – a union boss talking early, a detail in eulogy, SERT's deference, a shadow government minister briefed…

* * *

The round-up of Western Downs cops was led by Sergeant Vern Crous of the Miles Police Station. Miles is about the same distance to Wains Road as Chinchilla. Crous got word and put out a call to other stations. Two down, one wounded and one in deadly danger right now, saw 16 officers drop everything and go there. Other police manned the station phones and other communications in the three Downs stations involved. Coordinated liaison, the Brisbane-#251link, the trio links vital.

They were at #251 about 6.30 pm, two hours after the four tasked with the welfare check had arrived. Smoke rose from the torched police vehicle and the smouldering grass and scrub around the driveway.

Their first shock was the dead body of a civilian male lying in the shooters' driveway. Someone, probably a cop who had worked with the Rural Fire Brigade, recognised him as RFB volunteer Al Dare.

The priority job was to get Con Keely Brough to safety. How they found her before the grass fire did – journalist Candace Sutton thinks they were just in time – and how they got her out is unknown. Her relief to hear shots fired from *behind* her can only be imagined for now. Her body cam recording will no doubt be played at the inquest. 'If it wasn't for these officers… there'd be another young cop dead, Keely Brough,' said Shadow Police Minister Dale MP empathetically. But she *was* got out. Qld Opposition leader David Crisafulli MP said two days later in Tara that 'some incredible stories of bravery by our police are going to come out in the days ahead'.

The country cops got the bodies of Matthew Arnold and Rachael McCrow out from the fenced homestead area 'while being fired at continuously'[1] It was a bold, brave, beyond-the-call-of-duty action to take.

They were not done until the hand-over to the Special Emergency Response Team, SERT.

I can see no way Crous and team were able to do what they did without being able to pin down the Trains with their own gunfire. It is not doubted they were gutsy and brave, but turning up to face deadly armed ambushers without long arms is not something police would do.

Ian Leavers, Queensland Police Union president, was on the Western Downs very quickly, and talked to those local police before the QPS curtain came down. The Western Downs officers did not make a big deal of it to him, treated it as what you do; Leavers was nevertheless impressed. In a eulogy, as we will see, a salute: 'To Rachel's brothers in blue… thank you for not leaving our sister out there.' SERT officers, superbly fit, highly trained, men of multiple skills, confident, rejoicing in the status of an elite – their Victorians counterparts, the Special Operations Group, won't correct you when you suggest SOG stands for 'Sons Of God' – and in the way of elites, not given to modesty. But this team were magnanimous. 'Don't look at us, what about them?'[2] they said, directing the attention of the politician congratulating them to the country cops.

A few police valour medals seem appropriate when the coroner is through.

* * *

When the two Pol Air helicopters – Queensland Pol Air is helicopters and pilotless aircraft; fixed-wing are a separate part of the service – got there, we don't know. The QPS Bell 206 and MBB Bo 105 choppers can carry three or four passengers, the new Bell 429, five. These choppers can do reconnaissance, track, carry a litter and do many things, but acting as a troop carrier or as a gunship is out of the question. It may be the helicopters took a SERT member or two with them, perhaps dropping them off at a local airport – Tara's is closest, Chinchilla's close enough – where Pol Air could fuel up and perhaps where an advance SERT officer could join the local officers on Wains Road. When the choppers hovered over there, they were shot at.

The SERT got there at 9 pm. Their BearCat armoured vehicle is capable of highway speeds, the supplier specifying top speed 140 kph. Such teams usually have an expert negotiator with them. If SERT had one in this siege – and Commissioner Carroll has alluded to attempts made to persuade the murderous trio to surrender – they were working uphill because the perpetrators did not want to listen or survive. They wanted to kill and be killed.

At 9.30 SERT had broken through the perimeter fence and bought the Bearcat up to facilitate easier communication between the negotiator and those around the house. That the Bearcat took a lot of gunfire suggests the trio's reply. It returned to Brisbane on a tow truck.

There is much we do not yet know about the time between SERT's arrival and when the Trains were shot dead around 10.30 pm.

What we do know, because QPS released the audio to media three days later, is what happened in the last five minutes of the siege, what Pol Air said to SERT members on the ground.

Qld Pol Air dispatched two helicopters from Brisbane to the siege site. They were probably a Bell 206 or a MBB Bo 105, both single-jet turbine powered craft, or maybe one of their new twin-jet Bell 429s. Whichever, the operators need to be able to see above, below and over a wide angle each side, and sitting in a perspex bubble provides that. That is great for, say, the search and rescue of a sailor on a sinking yacht in high seas, but a vulnerability in a gunfight.

Brisbane to Wieambilla is about 180-200 km as the crow flies, flight time a little under an hour but with pre-flight checks and so on, a little over an hour before they got there. They get two hours aloft on a tank of fuel, so one probably peeled off to refuel at Tara, Chinchilla or Dalby airports, all of which supply jet A1, the kind of refined kerosene needed. From arrival, police kept an eye in the sky at all times. Aircraft safety dictated that they stayed high, at 3000 feet or more, turned off all lights and did not use their nightsun, capable of illuminating the ground with 3 million candlepower. They did not need it. The powerful video camera in the FLIR – Forward-Looking Infra-Red – system is capable of distinguishing a flat |from a Phillips X screw head on your numberplate, and has thermal imaging for night work. The communications system does not pick up the noise of the rotor blades or gunshots on the ground.[3]

'POI' is Person Of Interest, here the two males, POI 1 and POI 2. Stacey, distinguishable, is 'the female POI'. 'White side' is the approach to the house, 'black side' behind it, and 'red side' is where the stairs and couch are and where the 'the utility' was parked. The sun has long set. The house was under siege by local police and then SERT for nearly six hours. 'Laser' here refers to an option on the FLIR to place a marker dot on something or someone on the ground.

> Both POIs now weapons facing white side and as you see, they've got spotlight on top of the utility and discharging weapons white side.
>
> Single male discharging his weapon, so main POI discharging his weapon has moved to the rear of the utility. The second male is sitting on the stairs, red side stairs.
>
> From what I am looking at, the main POI is obtaining rounds and loading the weapon from the rear of the utility.

POI back open side driving door, weapons resting on the door. Weapons facing white side. Weapons discharging white side. Weapons discharging white side.

[Inaudible] I am not sure if you are getting my transmissions, but the offenders are on the red side and the weapons have discharged towards white side.

[Inaudible] so, the main POI is now at the rear of the utility, and it would appear he has a number of cartridges on the rear tray and that is where he is reloading his weapon.

Ahhh, unable to ascertain that. We're not getting a response from our laser. There have been no indicators.

The second male POI is sitting on the stairs on the red side access stairs. The female is unsighted, assumed to be [inaudible – inside?]

Polair to SERT, no change. POI 1 appears to be reloading weapons from the rear tray of the vehicle.

Polair to SERT, POI back at the driver's door, driver's door is open. POI remains outside the vehicle.

Polair to SERT, weapon is now facing white side. Weapon is back have discharged facing towards white side, copy?

Yeah, Pol Air 1, sorry, this is Pol Air 2. A number of shots going off there. Continuously every five seconds.

POI is now back rear tray of the vehicle and POI 2 remains on the red side stairs.

Polair to SERT, we are not sure, but he may have discharged a round toward black side. Unconfirmed.

Polair to SERT, second POI back at the couch facing white side and POI 1 back at the driver's side of the vehicle.

Polair to SERT, we're happy that we've seen a pair of legs on the red side balcony so assume that is the POI female.

Polair to SERT, POI 2 still moving.

Polair to SERT, POI 2 is now on his back.

Polair to SERT, POI 2 still [has] movement, still movement from POI 2.

Polair to SERT, no movement from number 1. Still movement from number 2.

Number 2 is still moving on the couch. Number 1, no movement.

Polair to SERT, no change. No movement from number 1.

Well [inaudible] on the [inaudible]

Polair to SERT, so we do have movement from number 2

To SERT, so female down. Face down.

Polair to SERT, two dogs coming white side, two dogs coming to you, white side.

Polair to SERT, there's still movement from number 2. Still movement from number 2 on the couch.

Polair to SERT, so shots fired from number 2 white side.

Polair to SERT, still have movement from number 2, he's on the couch on his back, facing directly upwards. Still has movement.

Polair to SERT, no change. Still movement from number 2. On his back, facing upwards.

Polair to SERT, so POI number 2 still discharging rounds. Number 1 and female are down. No movement. On the couch, still moving. On the couch, face towards white side. Still movement.

Polair to SERT, Number 2 on the couch. One [inaudible].

Two's moving, down on the ground beside the vehicle.

Standing up.

Number 2 is down. Still has movement. Dropping to the ground.

[Inaudible] had side of the vehicle.

Polair to SERT, he's down. [Inaudible] facing the vehicle, no movement.

Polair to SERT, we have movement on number 2. Number 2's not moving.

> Polair to SERT, still have movement on number 2. Down on the ground, laying on his left-hand side, behind the couch, facing the vehicle.
>
> Polair to SERT, no change. The movement has semi-reduced.
>
> Polair to SERT, I don't have movement.

It was shortly after 10.30 pm when the six-hour siege of 251 Wains Road ended in this way.

* * *

The police decision to shoot to kill was clearly taken late, as a last resort. It is clear the three Trains had decided to die by police bullet long before 12 December. An unacknowledged anonymous 'police source' is said to have said the trio were armed with 'farm guns' unequal to the task of a shoot-out. This takes too much notice of armoury and no enough of the deranged psychology that had been stewing on 251 Wains for months. In the light of Nathaniel's border breaching with guns and ammunition as his major cargo and the two men's preoccupation with weaponry, this suggests that they sought to beef up their firepower. Still, SERT had recourse to gear made for a situation such as a siege. SWAT, the general term for police quasi-military teams, means Special Weapons And Tactics: body armour, fire-resistant balaclavas, assault rifles, sub-machineguns, laser sights, night-sight googles, thermal-imaging scopes… the list goes on.

The Trains had a shotgun, a .22 LR (Long Rifle) with an effective range of 100 metres perhaps, and a 30-06 (*say* 'thirty-oh-six') rifle, a standard NATO infantry weapon for 50 years. Presumably this last was the weapon that put holes in the QPS's BearCat front window during the reported 90-minute gun 'battle' the Trains were predestined to lose.

A police source told *The Australian* Stacey Train was a willing participant, shooting at police. 'She got shot and went down and was still shooting at police as she was laying on the ground. She was then shot and killed.'

Acting Commissioner Tracy Linford, dealing with the debate on national gun laws, was able to clarify how the Trains had so much ammunition. Nathaniel simply purchased it locally – and legally. Queensland retailers are obliged to sight an up-to-date physical licence card with a photo of the holder and the class of weapon and therefore ammo, they are entitled to buy. Nathaniel alone among the trio had one, and he bought plenty and often. The murderous idiots at 251 were emboldened to make their theatrical suicidal end without running out of ammo and being taken alive. This alone makes Nathaniel as guilty as sin in the three murders.

QPS officers before 12 December had been unable to serve the firearms suspension notice arising from the firearms in the creek at the border. This meant he still had a valid card. As early as August 2022 police officers had gone to 251 Wains Road to serve a suspension notice to find the gate locked and cctv installed, not all that unusual on the Wieambilla blocks. One cop wrote on his card in front of the lens, waved it to camera, and made a show of putting it in the letterbox. He or she tried phoning – no dice. A QPS officer who later called at 251 found the card in the letterbox box still and concluded no-one had been at, or was at the address, a natural conclusion anywhere, and absences from home were not unusual on the blocks.[4]

* * *

Daybreak, 251 Wains Road. The first police to go on the Trains' domestic area followed police dogs sent in to sniff out any bobby traps that may have been set up. Given the perpetrators' elaborate defence-and-surveillance system and the advice on Improvised Explosive Devices available on some SovCit and prepper websites, sending in a K9 forward scout or two was a prudent move. The parallels with army patrol practice in occupied Iraq or Afghanistan and Iraqi and Taliban terrorist methods make a sobering comparison. SES volunteers formed lines, called emu parades in Australia, ostrich parades elsewhere, and walked the execution ground a yard or two apart, looking for evidence for police.

When the all-clear was given, crime scene and homicide police moved in, and the investigation began. Photography *in situ*. Markers laid as evidence bags filled. Bodies consigned to a morgue for autopsy. Computers and cameras removed for expert analysis. Etcetera. And so, the sad, methodical business goes…

1 Ian Leavers, 9news.com.au, 13 December 2022

2 Candace Sutton, *Daily Mail Australia,* 15 December 2022

3 Posts on-line to the effect that the QPS's audio is 'a fake' have relied on the lack of these. It is normal suppression of ambient sound for clear communication.

4 Rory Callinan, ABC News, 18 February 2023

13
The Victims

CONDOLENCE
TO THE 2 FALLEN
OFFICERS & THEIR
FAMILIES & FRIENDS
Matthew Arnold & Rachel McCrow
REST IN PEACE
– Placard worn by Danny Lim

I first heard about the Wieambilla shootings on the radio news while I was at my desk. I had previously published or written books on shootings of police.

In 1991 my company published Tom Noble's account of the murders of Victoria Police Constables Steven Tynan, 22, and Damian Eyre, 20, in the leafy inner-Melbourne suburb of South Yarra in 1988.[1]

The subsequent police investigation and trial did not cover itself with glory, and in the 2020s the Walsh Street murders are still unfinished business.

I remember how I first learned of that shooting. I suspect many Victorians have their personal hearing about it etched in their minds too.

I had a bookshop in Richmond. On Wednesday 12 October 1988 I had not heard any media news when I opened the door for trade for the day. In Melbourne in early Spring, a bloke feels he really ought to be outside.

(Well, I do.) I dawdled outside on the street after I set up, thought about washing the windows to stay out, and decided against it. Hanging about with my hands in my pockets, I saw a regular customer, a local I knew quite well, coming up the street.

'Gidday, Margaret. How're things?'

'Gidday. Isn't it terrible about those young policemen?'

'What young policemen?'

She told me that two cops had been shot dead in the middle of the night in South Yarra, the first suburb across the Yarra River from where we stood. 'One of them was only twenty. Twenty!'

Margaret was young as widows go. She was in a reflective mood and told me about the first and only time she had called for police assistance. Margaret was home alone in her apartment when a party, not for the first time, turned noisy and raucous next door. But the voices on that particular night had turned mean and ugly. Someone drunk was 'going to get some fucking money'. When her own door handle had twice been tried from without, she decided it was time to ring police. Two young Richmond police turned up, talked to her, went next door and told the partygoers to pull their heads in, returned to reassure her and advised her not to hesitate to ring again if there was further trouble. The shooting overnight had put her in mind of them again.

'They had no idea what was waiting for them behind my door, let alone next door.' She had belatedly become aware of the routine courage in what on-call police do all day and all night. Margaret was an intelligent, thoughtful person. A woman of the world, she known ups and downs, and death close to her, but I don't think policing was a subject she had given much thought before that day. Now this – two men shot down by somebody in the shadows for no apparent reason, but in cold blood.[2]

* * *

The big parallel common to the murders in Walsh Street and those first two in Wieambilla is the arbitrary nature of the selection of cop to die.

This breaks hearts: so young, so much promise, but in an instant, gone. Yet in the Train's gunsights, they are just cops. Cop equals target. Pull trigger. Cop dies. That's the horror at the core of it.

On the day after the Wieambilla crimes the Queensland Police Union had issued photographs of Rachael McCrow, 29, and Matthew Arnold, 26 to media. Two informal snaps.

Rachel's looked like it may have been snapped at her graduation ceremony. She is immaculate in blue serge slacks and cotton shirt. She is with a woman with an arm around her shoulders who looks like she could be Rachel's mum. Rachel has the beginnings of a smile on her face. Later photographs published showed she had a magic smile, a smile kissed by nature: broad, easy, warm, unaffected, beguiling… She's the girl next door who everybody would like next door. Over the next days, the QPS media unit would replace that snap, for the memorial service invitation for example, with one which showed more of that smile's sparkle and ditched the hat.

Matthew's photo showed him in a number 3 haircut and sporting an older-than-five-o'clock shadow, a hint of a brown-gingery beard, with a warm, open smile. He's dressed in on-duty kit, cop radio mouthpiece high on his chest and wearing the usual crowded-belt cop paraphernalia. And, to compound the viewers' warm sentiment (and sense of tragic waste), he's holding a puppy, which, on a second look, is two puppies. Other photos of Matthew emerged, but the union's first choice never wavered with the media unit.

Rachel and Matthew were housemates in a police-owned Tara house, and well-known, popular figures around town. Matthew had planned and packed to drive to Brisbane to have Christmas with his parents. Some reports said arrangements fell through when duty intervened, others that the arrangement stood until his tragic end. A local said remembered Matthew as 'always smiling'.

In Tara the focus of horror and sorrow was on the police station. There, 200 individuals, some openly teary, visited, to hug and console local and relieving coppers, express condolences, deliver messages they or their children had written, drop off flowers… Tara's population is about 2000!

In Chinchilla the florists' stocks were soon exhausted. The station there too was a place for sorry business. Assistant Commissioner Charysse Pond and Constable Keely Brough – Constable Randall Kirk was still in hospital – were there daytime and for the candlelit vigil held at the Illoura Village aged care and nursing home that night.

* * *

It fell to Commissioner Katrina Carroll APM to speak for the QPS and its people, the number of whom far exceed the 11,000 sworn officers. Her

Tuesday addresses to media camera from the Chinchilla Police Station took in their loved ones too.

> Matthew was sworn in as a police officer in March 2020, while Rachel was sworn in last year in June 2021... Losing one of our own has a profound impact on every single officer and their families. To lose two officers in one incident is absolutely devastating. This event is the largest loss of police life we have suffered in a single incident in many years.

Carroll had spoken by phone to, and said she would be visiting, Matthew and Rachel's devastated families. She had talked to Keely and arranged time with Randall when he was expected to exit hospital. She had been to 251 Wains Road. Of the people she commanded, she frankly acknowledged that their shock was giving way to hurting, that the coming days would be 'dark' and painful... but QPS would rally and would not forget Rachel and Mathew. Her words and demeanour suggested a frank, emotionally honest spokesperson. Questioned, she dampened down any suggestion that details would quickly emerge, said the investigations of the crime scene alone 'could take weeks'. I suspect she had had very little sleep but she had got to the right place, early, talked to key cops, contacted grieving families, and fronted all media comers. In 'the Job' that is a core part of the commissioner's job.

Queensland Police Union president Ian Leavers announced that a fundraiser had been set up for the Arnold and McCrow families.

> They were both amazing people who were well respected by their colleagues and those who were close to them... I spoke with Matthew's father last night. It's hard to know what to say. He was devastated... Our thoughts go out to Matthew's parents and Rachel's family as well.

Queensland's premier Annastacia Palaszczuk announced state flags would be lowered to half-mast, and some buildings, including Brisbane's

Storey Bridge, would be lit up in blue and white to commemorate the dead officers.

The tributes of organisations flowed. Queensland Cricket and Cricket Australia opened the Australia v South Africa First Test with a moving one at the Gabba. Police including Commissioner Carroll, sergeants and constables stood on the field under a scoreboard with portraits of Rachel and Matthew on it. A Yuggarra elder, dancer Aunty Deborah Sandy, paid tribute. A heartfelt speech introduced a minute's silence, hats and caps off among older spectators, players and police. Players wearing black armbands circulated among the visibly moved police, expressing personal condolences. The clapping of the crowd was enthusiastic and sustained.

The Sydney Opera House was turned blue too. Out and about in that city the irrepressible activist Danny Lim wore a new placard in remembrance.

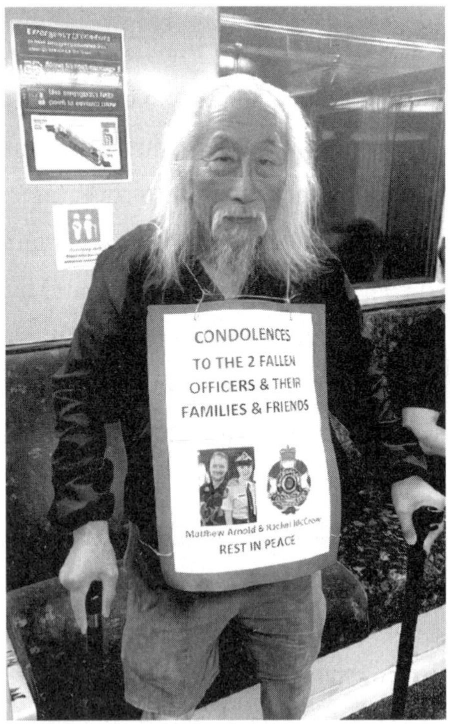

Danny Lim

This urge to make remembrance spread throughout a shocked and saddened nation.

* * *

The Queensland Police Service laid on spit and polish, pomp and ceremony for the joint memorial service from 10 am Wednesday, 21 December. The service was held in the huge Brisbane Entertainment Centre, a big enough space to accommodate the 8000 ticketed mourners. The event was relayed to 11 screens across the state, including Tara, Chinchilla and Dalby on the Western Downs. It was livestreamed on the QPS Facebook page. ABC News, 7 and Nine channels broadcast it.

Constables Keely Brough and Randall Kirk sat in the sea of fellow officers, some them former officers breaking out the old uniform from the closet.

Prime Minister Anthony Albanese and Leader of the Opposition Peter Dutton (a QPS officer in the 1990s) and Premier Annastacia Palaszczuk, Police Minister Mark Ryan and Leader of the Opposition David Crisafulli attended, along with Governor Dr Jeannette Young

Representatives of every state and territory police, the NYPD and FBI and attended.

QPS Chaplain Jeffery Baills had been talking to the Arnold and McCrow families beforehand, and he addressed them directly from the speaker's podium. He said 'What happened on December 12 was un-Australian and does not belong in this country. It was absolute evil. This barbaric act has shocked our country and it's irreparably damaged you.'

Otherwise, the killers might as well not have ever existed.

Premier Palaszczuk mentioned Alan Dare's motives and actions.

Commissioner Katarina Carroll outlined the professional biography, Statement of Service, of the deceased. Medals, national and state, to the two families seated in the front row, were conferred, wreathes laid.

Two colleagues who knew the slain officers were heard in eulogy.

Senior Sergeant Laura Harriss, friend of the Arnold family, called Mathew Joseph Arnold 'brave, loyal and kind', a charmer, charismatic, a big brother, a leader and, riffing on a hope his parents had expressed to him, noting he was tall and that people would *have* look up at him, they hoped he would also be one that people *wanted* to look up to. She declared him a success in that.

Senior Constable Melissa Gibson described her 'mate Rach' as a 'cheeky larrikin who loved a laugh, loved a good prank and loved a good meme, often at our expense'; recalled Rachel's winning smile, positive attitude, listening skills and 'warmest of hearts'. She spoke of Rachael's admiration of her mother, who seems to have brought Rachael and her sister up solo. Archibald, Rachel's blue heeler, got a mention too

She also alluded to an act of courage by '16 country cops' that fatal day mentioned only once before, with admiration, by the union's man in the immediate aftermath, before police brass zipped all police lips. 'To Rachel's brothers in blue, who showed an enormous amount of courage to go in and bring her out, thank you for not leaving our sister out there.' How local cops got the bodies out under fire is a story that remains to be told.

Constable Freddy Hartigan, part of Intake 44 with Rachel at the Townsville academy, too praised her ability to listen, helpfulness, academic and sportive dedication, thanked her for a peek at her pre-exam notes, and revealed she had an aim to get into the QPS Child Protection and Youth Justice Unit one day. He felt she could have made commissioner rank.

Archibald, Rachael's well-behaved blue heeler, had the back seat of a police car all to himself going to the service, window half open, head and tongue out. He sat quietly on a loose lease during it. And he walked out in the procession onto Melaleuca Drive with his cop minder in behind his best friend's coffin. The cops have a protocol for most things, but I doubt there's a sub-section called 'Pet Dogs'. What they did, seems apt to me: she loved him *and* she taught him well. Things no doubt reciprocated.

The hearses moved through a guard of honour 1000 metres long. They were followed by bagpipers at slow march, police on horses, the K9 squad with their dogs, a motorcycle escort, water police and their boats on ponds, and, above them, Polair choppers. Commissioner Katarina Carroll commands nearly 12 000 sworn officers and 3600 unsworn staff. This was a day for inclusion. The heart, mind and the soul of the department all demanded it.

In Chinchilla old-timer Graham Stewart from the nearby hamlet of Brigalow had been thinking – and talking – about an old custom: as the funeral procession passed, shopkeepers used to shut up their shops and stand in the street. 'Why,' he asked, 'don't we do that? Doesn't matter that it is in Brisbane.' And so, it was done again, among the laurel trees on Chinchilla's main street that Wednesday. They could of course watch on their phones or wander over to the big screen.

And from the eulogies, family slideshows and messages, we who watched got an idea of what these flesh-and-blood individuals were like.

Rachael had studied (an ex-Genesis Christian College girl from Moreton Bay), travelled, and worked at the Queensland Crime and Corruption Commission before joining intake 44 at the Townsville Police Academy, where she shone and graduated in June 2022. A generous student, she had organised study sessions and runs at dawn among intake 44. She was a keen swimmer, insisting that a cast on her broken arm be waterproofed so she could continue to start the day with a dip in the sea or a workout in the pool. Her first post was at Dalby, her second of course Tara. Her hopes and dreams can be guessed from her family's selection of Daryl Braithwaite's 'Horses' and colleagues' references to her 'warm heart' and kind nature.

Matthew's family selected Luke Combs' country-and-western hymn to life, growing up, family and friends, and good memories 'Refrigerator Door'. I thought he had a blue heeler called Archibald (who was in photographs), and a three-syllable name for a dog suggested a quirky sense of humour. But of course, Archibald was his housemate Rachel's dog. He too first served in Dalby. Matthew was one of triplets, Hayley and James his siblings, but took on a 'big brother' role among the trio. He was somewhat of a high-school star at the crease in cricket, and most certainly a volleyball one. On his high-school graduation his parents, Terry and Sue, wrote him a letter outlining their general hopes for, and advice to him – *have* to and *want* look up to… comes from that letter. In the customary form of such a rite, Matthew replied: 'Thank you for everything. I may be gone someday. Soon, perhaps. But just know that I will never leave you. I will cherish every moment we've had together in my heart forever.'

(Hayley has since recalled, to *Queensland Police News*, a little of what it was like for the Arnold family on that awful Monday when they learned that a shooting incident in the area involving police was underway. Anxious, they tried ringing Matthew's cell phone. No dice. Hayley looked at her watch. She and Matthew shared each other's daily fitness inputs via an app. She learned he had taken 7000 steps since midnight Sunday, maybe traversed 500 metres that day, and was, at the time of her checking in, not moving. The gloom and the cruel closing aperture for hope can surely be imagined.)

Observance was not over for the McCrow and Arnold families and inner circles. Separate family funerals followed. Private ones.

* * *

Alan Dare's send-off was remarkable too, and very different.

A service with a celebrant took place in Ipswich, his hometown.

He was a self-confessed Ford fanatic and there are a lot of them like him in that respect in and around Ipswich apparently. Either that, or widespread respect for what he did and the injustice that he died for it, among those with a suitable car, got their motors running. Alan's funeral train had 25 kilometres of bright, shiny Ford muscle cars, hard tops and soft tops, in low gear, and a modest police motorcycle escort as well as aa fire truck; he was a volunteer firefighter. His widow Kerry, wife for 26 years, rode in a blue Ford Cobra XC, Al's favourite among the favoured.

Kerry and Al first meet when she was 10 and he 17, through her friendship with Al's sister and their two families lived four blocks from each in Leichhardt, but she was 30 and a mother when they married. He seems to have had a good bond with his dad, an army veteran of the Vietnam War. He was Al, Poppy Al and Rambo in his new family. She recounted with affection how they could sit together in companionable silence on their block, how the ex-meatworker loved the peace the place offered (and freedom from the relentless, repetitive, monotonous production-line work of meatworks no doubt). His stepson, Cory Richards, echoed a common thread among those who knew him: Al Dare was 'a quiet achiever'.

Kerry said, 'He built our house with his own hands and was ready to tell people "Come look, see what I've done"... I'm not sad about his life, he had a f***ing wonderful life.'[3]

Along the route to the Centenary Memorial Gardens in Brisbane southwest, kids he had never met held placards they had made. One had photographs of Racheal, Matthew and Alan with the message:

IN LOVING

Memory

Our Hero

Alan Dare

The ceremonials at the Gardens were low key and moving. Police Commissioner Katarina Carroll, solo, in uniform, attended. Kerry, their stepdaughter Renee, stepson Corey, and some of Alan's mates all paid heartfelt, fitting tributes. A grandson, 6 or 7 years old I guess, was lifted to the microphone and stole the show with his succinct prepared one: 'He was a very brave man, he was very strong and he was my best poppy ever.' Whitney Houston's soul number evoking the jazz torch-singer style, 'I Will Always Love You', was played. An apt poem ending with a couplet epitomising men like Alan Dare was read out and printouts circulated:

They don't show off…

They show up

Corey promised his shade, 'We're always going to be there, we're always going to look after mum.'

He was early dubbed 'Good Samaritan' after the man who helped the beaten-up stranger in the parable, Luke 10:30–37. That's fair.

The Queensland government paid for his funeral.

At the time of writing, more tributes to Alan Dare are planned. In mid-January he received a police bravery award from Commissioner Carroll. A GoFundMe campaign raised at last count over $100,000 for Kerry and his family. Something about this happy, humble, honest, helpful, reliable man touched a lot of hearts.

* * *

There are less obvious victims of that place and day than the dead.

Two should not be forgotten: Randall Kirk and Keely Brough. The Chinchilla constables saw their colleagues jump a fence and get cut down by totally unexpected gunfire.

Kirk's instinct saw him go for the police van and radio, so the shooters zero-ed in on him. The nature of his leg wound is not clear, whether grazed by a bullet or hit by shotgun pellets or pierced by shrapnel. He made it into the vehicle, which took a lot of rifle fire. Somehow, he survived and drove out of range. His next acts were about letting cops know, in some reports by phone.

The shooters' focus on killing the mobile Randall Kirk escaping their trap may be what gave Keely Brough the window of opportunity to escape death. She did not run to the vehicle taking fire. What she did next – by instinct, brains and luck, her story to tell how much of each – was hit the dirt and look for a hiding place in the scrub around the driveway. She must have found wriggle-room-enough to get somewhere away from where the shooters last saw her upright. As described elsewhere, she hid like a prey animal in scrub, even when the Trains set the grass and bush on fire, like human hunters seeking food sometimes do. She may have witnessed Rachael and Matthew's shot at close range by police pistol. Plucky, Keely rang police, texted a family contact, faced the close possibility of death by bullet or fire with clarity and even some style, and considered wriggle-wriggle-then-walk to Robbs Road… Then the local cops arrived. And that changed everything.

Randall underwent surgery to remove metal from his leg. He issued a statement, 'bit sore but…', expressed condolences, thanked everyone 'from the Prime Minister down' and asked for privacy for himself and his wife Breanna and the child that were expecting to be born in the January just around the corner.

Much has been made of their youth – 28 and 29 years – and rookie-hood, particularly Keely, only eight or nine weeks out of the police academy. Looks to me, the academy taught them well. After all, all the odds were with the shooters who wanted them dead, and they are alive.

They apparently got mental-health help. An experience like theirs on that Monday will leave scars that will need time to heal.

* * *

When Commissioner Carroll called the murders of Constables McCrow and Arnold the 'largest loss of police life we [Queensland police] have suffered in a single incident in many years', later in 'over 100 years', she was she on the right horse: the murders of John Power and Patrick Cahill. Queensland is no stranger to the shooting of police in cold blood.

Thomas Griffin served in the Royal Irish Constabulary, soldiered in the Crimean War, and returned to Britain a decorated war hero. He sailed to Victoria and married a woman who he thought was a rich widow. She was apparently not rich enough for his flamboyant expenditure. He deserted her, apparently leaving her with legally binding IOUs to pay.

He wound up in Rockhampton, a port on what today is called the Queensland Central Coast. After the Colony of Queensland was carved out of the Colony of New South Wales, alluvial gold was discovered inland, in places like Clermont. As Griffin was Rockhampton's Chief Constable, a police magistrate, Gold Commissioner to the Clermont diggings, and socially and politically well-connected locally, he was sitting pretty.

Some say he laid bets on credit in Chinese gambling dens; others say he was entrusted with the safekeeping of six Chinese digger's gold to the agreed value of £252 and failed to pay up on call because he had gambled it away. Today, he would be called a 'problem gambler'. Furthermore, news of his desertion of his wife down south had travelled to the Tropic of Capricorn. A Rockhampton woman of influence threatened to cut him locally. He needed ready money fast.

An escort was arranged to leave Rockhampton, where the banks were, carrying by horseback bank notes and gold bullion to the tune of £4,000 to go 380 km to the Clermont diggings. There, they would pick up diggers' assayed gold dust to take back to Rockhampton's banks. Gold Commissioner Thomas Griffin, 35, offered his experience and guidance to OIC Sergeant Julian and the two young rookies who were to escort the cash and gold.

Australians have never acknowledged that their early policemen were overwhelmingly Irish. New Yorkers made the Irishness of the local cops, the New York Police Department, a literary, filmic and pop culture icon. In Victoria and Western Australia, the predominance of Irishmen in police ranks far exceeded that of the New York. It will become obvious to readers that I think Ned Kelly was a very ordinary type of rural petty criminal, but the cold-blooded killing of cops makes him a scumbag, not a hero. Nevertheless, his pen portrait of the Victoria Police as 'a parcel of big ugly fat-necked wombat-headed big-bellied magpie-legged narrow-hipped splaw-footed sons of Irish Bailiffs or English landlords' – when stripped of his admittedly memorable insults and knee-jerk rebel Irish bigotry – is ethnically spot on. This letter had a *zing!* to it, and newspaper sub-editors called 'Copy boy! Front page, tell 'me!' And readers' joy then and since has made Ned Kelly Australia's most well-known folk hero. I feel lonely dissenting. The big difference between the Gareth Train's on-line raves and Ned Kelly's Jerilderie Letter rave is that Kelly's is a coherent rave. There is nothing in Train's rave that is memorable. His words and images may make headlines when the coroner's court sits, but his words and images will be quickly forgotten.

The rookies on the escort were Constables John Power, 25, and Patrick Cahill, 27. They knew each other as schoolboys on a county border in southern Ireland. John was a smiling, almost six-foot tall, blond-haired guy. Patrick too was tall and blond. Power had worked in Victoria and NSW, but not as a policeman. They met up again, as far as can now be figured, by happenstance in Central Queensland in 1865. Patrick had a police job in the new breakaway colony as a gold escort officer and he told Power to apply to be one too. Power did and got the gig.

The horse train left Rockhampton in uniform – slouch hats, riding boots, what looks like military khaki in the old black-and-white pictures, but not blue – and carbines, the rifle of choice for mounted men everywhere by 1867. Not far into the journey Sergeant Julian accused Griffin of trying to poison him, and rode back to Rockhampton alone. Griffin, Power and Cahill plugged on west, to the Crossing on the Mackenzie River, and struck camp there though Griffin booked into the nearby bush pub called Bedford Hotels for the night.

Next morning the innkeeper said he heard shots fired during the night. Griffin said that's be his troopers shooting dingos. He left for Rockhampton, clearly without visiting the camp on the Crossing.

John Power and Patrick Cahill died on the riverbank that night, 5 November 1867, and a bushman found their bodies a day or two later.

The news that they were dead, and a fortune was missing quickly reached Rockhampton. Early reports had it that the two young officers had died of 'poisoning'. Two pigs had been found nearby, trotters pointing at the sky, dead as door nails; so, perhaps there was a bit of poison about? What amounted to a posse – Sergeant Julian, an inspector, a detective, a bank manager, Dr Salmon and Gold Commissioner James Griffin – left Rockhampton for the Crossing at speed. The cash and gold, and the bank's and port of Rockhampton's hopes of a road to prosperity, demanded action.

The medic pointed out that the young guys had clearly died of a gunshot wound to the head. No 'poison' was found. In the days when Dr Salmon was putting his post-mortem point of view forward, 'poison' meant toxins, chemicals that can make you sick, that can kill you. In the circumstances Dr Salmon faced then, he volunteered this: no *toxin* does not rule out a narcotic. *Narcotic* is a sleep-inducing drug. Opiates were the paracetamol of the day, sold over the counter everywhere from the 1860s on, and there was no test for the presence of opiates back then. Dr Salmon thought the two young men would have been out to it when they took execution-style bullets to the head, the second victim oblivious to the noisy death of the first. James Griffin was arrested on two charges of murder on the spot.

In court, he pleaded not guilty: it was bushrangers what did it. The prosecution's case was, though circumstantial, had strong circumstance to kill for money. The jury: 'Guilty.' The judge put the black patch of fabric over his horsehair wig, as was the form when sentencing a convicted person to death.

Thomas Griffin confessed. He had lifted consignment cash first in Rockhampton before departure. He was hanged in the Rockhampton Gaol, 1 June 1868. The bent cop killer has not had his name etched on the National Police Memorial in Canberra. But Cons John Power and Patrick Cahill have.

Commissioner Carroll was well-informed, and when she said QPS 'will never forget' Rachel and Matthew she spurred me to re-tell this 155-year-old story. I suspect someone in the year 2177 may, out of some unhappy parallel, re-tell theirs.

1*Walsh Street: the cold-blooded killings that shocked Australia* 1991 which later was the basis of the feature film *Animal Kingdom*. I later co-wrote, with Ray Mooney, *A Pack of Bloody Animals: Walsh Street revisited*, 2011

2 John Kerr, *Cop Killers*, Melbourne, 2010

3 Peter Gunned & others, ABC News 23 December 2022

14
Aftershocks and Ripples

I received a message from my brother Daniel, and my sister Jane, in Queensland, Australia, but the devils came for them, to kill them. And they had to kill the devils themselves and are now on the run... These are people that are not armed as we are in America. Here my brave brother and sister have done what they are supposed to do, and kill these devils... [last words Stacey spoke to him, Biblical verse:] 'Where there is a corpse, the vultures will gather.'

– 'Don' aka Geronimo's Bones, from videos posted online 12–16 December 2022

'Don' (see epigraph above) was favoured with what Stacey Train knew would be her last known words, favoured over her own daughter, whose SMS text of concern went unanswered in the besieged house.

The self-appointed preacher in Arizona video-ed his reflections standing in what looks like snow glare, beanie pulled low, jacket zipped up high, black nose ring bobbing and raving about how much he loved the Wieambilla killers and hates almost everyone else, using the word 'fucking' like a comma.

The Federal Bureau of Investigation have promised the Queensland Police assistance with the investigation, so 'Don' can expect a call from them. It may begin with 'Put your fucking hands above your fucking head, motherfucker.' As Don put it himself, 'The only language that evil ever respects, responds to, or understands is the language of virtuous violence.'

* * *

In the Central Downs, where the loss of life was personal for many, and especially for deeply scarred local police and the Dare family, the necessary emotional business of grieving and healing was an intense business. At the Miles Police Station, where Rachael had spent a time before her posting to Tara, Senior Constable Scott Pogan decided the Big Blue Gang could do with a bit of green therapy and a small memorial garden at the front door of the cop shop would include the community. A plot was dug, bordered, planted out and two cut rocks with etched plagues erected.[1] Solar-powered lights will still be shining on that garden in the dark of night long after the video clip of Geronimo's Bones is forgotten.

* * *

Gerard Gill has worked with The Global Network on Extremism & Technology and wandered in the cesspools of conspiracist blogs, posts, forums and the like more than most. He notes that premillennialism is not necessarily an extremist belief (nor confined only to Christians), but 'it blends in with... conspiracist thinking'.

What Gill says about premillennialism is correct and important. I too believe religiously motivated violent extremism blended with ideologically motivated violent extremism in Wieambilla. But to me premillennialism is such pure baloney, I should leave you with the more patient Dr Gill awhile. [2]

'Then, you might see [the apocalypse] as something that's happening now and you might think you need to take extreme action.' Citing research associating premillennialism with violent and extreme propensities, he says it 'heightens the stakes for things, it allows you to see the world in a very black-and-white way. It's a point of no return that certain people are the devil, and certain people are of God...'

'For the big players in the freedom movement, [the Wieambilla shootings] slowed them down for a day, but they believed that they weren't responsible. They threw out that it was a false flag and kept promoting conspiracies.'[3]

Business as usual in the cesspools.

* * *

The first positive ripple out of the Wieambilla shootings was that there should be a national firearm register, an NFR.

The logic as it pertained to the four cops who attended 251 Wains Road is impeccable. Before setting out on the welfare check, they could have consulted the NFR database and established there was a history of registered firearms in the hands of the Train brothers. Whether it would made any difference – the Trains' licensed guns were common farm ones, not AK47s or M16s – is unknowable.

If such an NFR had been operating for a quarter of a century, they might have known that in 1998 in Queensland, Gareth Train was charged with unlawful firearm possession (he did not renew registration), and that the missing person they sought was a suspended registered gun owner in New South Wales. We are now sadly aware there were six firearms at 251, two unregistered, four registered in two states.

That 'quarter of a century' is not rhetoric. In 1996 Arthur Bryant in Port Arthur, Tasmania became the world's then most prolific shooter of people in peacetime. It turned out to be Prime Minister John Howard's finest hour. The PM appeared at meeting full of gun owners and gun enthusiasts in Sale, Victoria wearing a flak jacket under his suit, for which he was criticised, a criticism that seems naïve, even laughable, today. He instituted a gun amnesty and people turned in their guns– aged urban widows getting rid of their late husbands' farm or hunting rifle was a big and harmless part of the over 1 million guns handed in and crushed, but some were military or quasi-military weapons and handguns.

The National Firearms Agreement 1996 became federal law but few were happy with it. In 2002 there was a horrific random shooting killing on the campus of Monash University in Victoria. But the government in Canberra had moved onto other things, work on a national registry simply did not proceed and Australia had eight registries with different rules, categories, systems, then and now. The number of registered guns has risen steadily over the last 20 years, but the number of registered owners has dropped dramatically: more own more than one gun, some many more, now.

After security chief Mike Burgess raised the alt-right mad-man lone-wolf theoretical threat in 2022, followed by the hideous fact of the Wieambilla killings, there has been movement on the station. Prime Minister Anthony Albanese and state premiers had a link-up and pow-wow, Premier Annastacia Palaszczuk pushing a NFR hard. WA's Mark McGowan agreed, calling it a 'no-brainer'. Eight police ministers have been tasked with talking to each other and hammering out the details by mid-year. In early April 2023 the federal attorney-general Mark Dreyfus chaired an extraordinary meeting.

Ian Leavers, Queensland Police Union and Police Federation of Australia president, has called it time 'to pick up where John Howard left off'. Gun clubs, the Sporting Shooters Association of Australia and the Gun Safety Alliance are largely supportive. An Australian Health Promotion Association spokesperson called it 'long overdue'.

Gun Control Australia, a Not-for-Profit volunteer organisation dedicated to 'safe communities living without fear of gun violence' has long campaigned for a national uniform code, pointing out for example that silencers being OK in NSW but not in Queensland is dumb. (And a black-market opportunity.) To inform public debate, they pressed the Queensland government to release more information about the guns at 251 Wains Road. GCA's Roland Browne: 'they've now said that at least one of the guys had a gun licence, that three of the guns were registered to him and there were also a number of guns that weren't'. [4]

Prime Minister Anthony Albanese hoped to have made progress by the middle of the year on implementing an NFR, and on updating and review of terrorism laws promised by Home Affairs Minister Clare O'Neil. He said: 'That work is certainly under way…'

The department of the Federal Attorney General, Mark Dreyfus MP, ran public consultations in April 2023 and received 86 submissions from gun owners, industry, safety advocacy groups and academics. On 9 June police ministers recommended options for a NFR to the national cabinet, and Cabinet will announce and publish their deliberations. For police officers in particular and citizens in general – think of Alan Dare – the sooner the better. It would be sad, and could prove tragic, if a NFR was to wither on the vine again.

* * *

Police deaths arising from duty are always sad and bad. Obvious, but it needs said.

About 5 pm on a Wednesday afternoon in April 2020 two highway patrol officers pulled over the driver of a Porsche doing 140 kph on the Eastern Freeway in Melbourne. He, Richard Pusey, was about to make himself Victoria's Most Despised Man of 2020 for the disrespect he showed for police. He tested positive for MDMA and cannabis, and the police called for a hand in impounding his car. A police car, two officers, turned up.

A 19-tonne semi-trailer strayed into the emergency lane at 100 kph. Mohinder Singh, who had not slept for 67 hours out of the previous 72, was on methamphetamine and cannabis, and had babbled about seeing stick figures and was being chased by witches earlier that day, was behind the wheel. He plowed into a patrol vehicle first. In the following mayhem Senior Constable Kevin King, and Constables Lynette Taylor, Glen Humphris and Josh Prestney died.

Victoria Police had once before lost three officers in a single incident, the shooting murders by the Kelly Gang, and if you think Victoria Police had forgotten them, visit the scene of those crimes at Stringybark Creek where a plague dedicated to the memory of Sergeant Michael Kennedy, and Constables Michael Scanlon and Thomas Lonigan was installed and unveiled in 2001. The four at the Eastern Freeway truck crash was a melancholy police record, and one very nearly equalled at Wieambilla, lest we forget.

In the tad over a quarter of century to 2007, 22 Australian police were shot and died as a result. Of course, one is too many, but their union umbrella organisation, the Police Federation of Australia, has 66 000 members. Recruiters can look applicants in the eye and say the odds of being shot dead in 'the Job' are extremely low.

The Farm, forestry and fishing sector jobs kill by far the most people, year in, year out. The Construction, and the Road and rail sectors vie most years for # 2 and # 3 place. In fact, the Administrative and public safety sector, which covers policing never seems to be in the top ten sectors for fatalities. It is true police put their lives on the line every time they go on duty, but so do, say, taxi drivers.

Yet the malign intention or desperation of shooters of police will always trump cool industrial fatality statistics.

* * *

What police fear most about shooters is the ambush, what killed Brett Forte, Rachael, and Matthew. No, or not enough, warning.

Here we look at an ambush, the lessons for police and what was done.

'About 12.35 a.m. on 9 July 1995,' reads the touchstone of Robert Addison and Peter Spears, 9B of the National Police Memorial, beside the lake in Kings Park Canberra, 'the Constables were performing night shift at the Kempsey Police Station when they were called to a malicious damage complaint at the nearby township of Crescent Head. Having attended one address in relation to the complaint, they drove to a dwelling in Main Street Crescent Head. There they parked the Police vehicle in a driveway and began to walk toward the front door...'

The malicious damage was paint sprayed in anger on Ms Debra Minett's car by a drunk ex-, John McGowan, who had threatened to kill her on the phone, so she had rung police. The constables left her place to front McGowan at his.

The cops did not expect to confront him in his front yard armed with a Ruger .223, a gas-operated bolt-action self-loader, capable of a rapid rate of fire, of sending high-velocity .223 bullets out at will. Just squeeze the trigger. The cops had the then traditional Australian cop kit, a holstered six-shot .38 Smith & Wesson revolver on the belt. McGowan had dressed up: balaclava, hessian cape, camo-pants with the obligatory knife accessory, rifle cut down to a pistol grip and painted in camouflage colours: a Rambo suit.

McGowan yelled and charged at them. They retreated to their van. Spears, on foot, may have told McGowan to drop the gun. Addison seems to have made the van; he got off a radio request for urgent back up. The first shot McGowan fired hit the strut of the front window. Shooting became confused then, over 30 rounds fired. Peter Spears received a severe wound to the head and collapsed near the police 4WD. Addison got 'man down' message off, but because of communications problem in the area, he may not have known whether he had transmitted successfully or not. He also did know if Peter was dead or alive. Addison was shooting, yelling, 'Drop the gun. Put the gun down, John. Drop the gun.'

Addison sprinted across the road to reach a house phone, but that place was locked up. He shot the lock off, entered, but the empty dwelling did not have the phone on, a very unlucky short straw to draw in the mid-1990s. Bob Addison went back out.

A neighbour, Gregory Barnett, saw more of what happened next than anyone did. Though he spent most of the night lying on the bathroom floor with the rest of his family, he crawled out on his veranda at grave personal risk to help Bob. As Addison was trying to reload using a six-shot 'speed strip' he fumbled. The ammo fell to the ground in the dark. His torch went on.

McGowan rose on to one knee and fired. His bullet hit Bob in the chest, killing him.

By 1.20 a.m. McGowan had shot a pet dog. All the local dogs were howling. Sirens were wailing. The murderer was heard to say, 'I am sorry, I am sorry. I shot a policeman. Tell mum and dad I love them. Forgive me, God.' Then he turned the rifle on himself and the electrical linesman put out his own lights.

Asked later in court about the firefight, neighbour Gregory Barnett said, 'John had a cannon and they had shanghais.'

The cops' union, the NSW Police Association, wanted Glock pistols. That Robert Addison was found dead with an emptied gun chamber put a new urgency into their quest. The speed strip is easy enough to load on a training range in good light and out of danger, but the simplicity of a 15-shot magazine, and a snap to reload, made the *desirability* of the automatic a no-brainer.

NSW Police got Glocks in 1997-8. And the idea patrol vehicles should carry bullet-proof vests was advanced. NSW Police purchased 2000, $750 apiece, $1.5 million all up.

There are no happy endings in stories about cop killed on duty, but this one has the gift of a sweetener.

Peter's daughter Jade, 15, met Robert's son Craig, 16, and they really liked each other. Of course, they experienced different losses, but they shared their feelings of a deep sudden sadness inflicted on them in their mid-teens. They continued to like each other after their grief had ebbed, that attraction endured and, against the odds of teen romances, they stayed together to marry and have two sons. In 2003 it was reported that two police caps hung in their hallway, while family life bustled about when Blake was two and Joe just new.

The lesson from the Addison and Spears murders was that the Smith & Wesson had been become outdated. Maybe, but only maybe, a Glock could have saved the life of Robert Addison. But Peter Spears' life? Not in this ambush.

The two-year political and legal fight to get Glocks involved union representation at the inquest, Workcover NSW, the Industrial Commission, legal action under the Occupational Health & Safety Act, ballistics tests and a research paper, letter to Premier Bob Carr and much else I have spared you here. Police Department had budgetary restraints, an investment in .38 gear, and in-house lawyers. Furthermore, these department-union stoushes were repeated in other states, Victoria rolling out 10 000 Glocks costing $7 million in 2010, the last state to switch. There are no statistics on how many cop's lives Glocks saved; what doesn't happen, preventions, are beyond stats' reach.

Ambush favours the ambusher. They choose the time and place to shoot, a huge advantage, multiplied if they have time to prepare and conceal themselves. Glocks were no use to Brett Forte and team, or to the Wieambilla four.

Access to a firearm registry, even a good state one, might have saved Bob and Peter's lives. If they had access to a phone to a duty officer at Kempsey and rang through to get a check on John McGowan, they would have learned he had a licence to a Ruger .233 which he had allowed to lapse (reshaping the butt to a pistol grip is illegal, so he could not renew). The cops, and McGowan's ex-, had no idea McGowan had so much as a shanghai.

* * *

Australian Federal and state police have specific intelligence branches. Policing is dependent on keeping an ear to the ground, good local community connections and relations, registered informers, keeping files up to date, and sharing what is known with other, relevant groups. When it comes to domestic terrorism, one of those groups may be the Australian Security Intelligence Organisation, ASIO, and the sharing is mutual.

The Director-General of Security of ASIO, Mike Burgess, delivered his Annual Threat Assessment 2023 on 21 February 2023 and after preliminaries, addressed onshore threats:

> Late last year, I lowered the national domestic terrorism threat level from PROBABLE to POSSIBLE. This decision was not taken lightly or made casually.
>
> ASIO assesses that Australia remains a potential terrorist target, but there are fewer extremists with the intention to conduct an attack onshore than there were when we raised the threat level in 2014.
>
> This does not mean the threat is extinguished. Far from it.
>
> When making the announcement, I said it remained entirely plausible there would be a terrorist attack in Australia within

12 months, and that our biggest concern was individuals and small groups who could move to violence without warning, using weapons such as guns.

Tragically, all that came true just a few weeks later.

The horrific Wieambilla case demonstrates how, even with a lower threat level, the counter-terrorism mission remains challenging and the operational tempo is not diminishing.

Significant challenges and changes in the onshore security environment are adding to its complexity.

The reach of extremist content online means individuals are radicalising very quickly – in days and weeks – so the time between flash to bang is shorter than ever.

The radicalisation of minors is another concerning trend.

Terrorism remains a significant threat in some parts of the world and an emerging menace in others, and developments overseas could resonate here in Australia.

In our near region, under Islamic State of Iraq and the Levant's [ISIL's} influence, religiously motivated violent extremists are adapting their methods, with suicide bombings becoming more common in the southern Philippines, as well as attacks by females and families in the region more broadly.

Despite strong counter-terrorism pressure in the Philippines and Indonesia, ISIL-aligned violent extremists will continue to plan and conduct simple, often opportunistic attacks, primarily directed against local security forces and sectarian targets over the next six months.

More globally, we are following terrorism hotspots in Africa, the Middle East and South Asia. These are places where Australians live and work, where we have business interests and travel.

All of these factors mean ASIO cannot take its eye off the

ball and will continue to work with national and international partners to disrupt terrorism.

It is almost guaranteed that there will be a moment when a Director-General of Security will be standing here to advise that the domestic terrorism threat level is being raised again.

For now, though, the level remains at POSSIBLE – and that's despite the slaying of two police officers and a civilian in Wieambilla.

On behalf of ASIO, I again express my sincere condolences to the families of those killed, and Queensland Police more broadly. We work closely with many excellent officers in the Joint Counter-Terrorism Team, and I know how deeply these losses are felt.

ASIO worked with Queensland Police to assess what motivated the murderers, and we reached independent but identical conclusions.

We believe the shooting was an act of politically motivated violence, primarily motivated by a Christian violent extremist ideology.

Given the matter is still being investigated, I will refrain from going into more detail about ASIO's assessment other than to say we did not find evidence the killers embraced a racist and nationalist ideology or were Sovereign Citizens, despite their anti-authority and conspiracy beliefs.

It's disappointing some commentators and self-proclaimed terrorism experts were so quick to make definitive declarations about motivations, ideologies and political alignments in the immediate aftermath of the tragedy.

Proper, sober, accurate assessments require time and multiple inputs, including intelligence.

That's why ASIO is the authority on domestic threats. We have a unique role in the intelligence community. We are collectors and assessors, as well as disruptors. Our advice does not just

> draw on open-source material, we also have access to information obtained through ASIO's investigative and operational activity, and from our domestic and international partners. ASIO's experts weigh all available information, and use structured analytical techniques to test, retest and contest their assumptions.
>
> Speaking more generally, I'm also concerned that all too often commentators fail to distinguish between extreme views and violent extremism. One can lead to the other, but that does not mean they are the same thing. It takes careful, nuanced work to disentangle groups and individuals that will engage in violence, from groups and individuals that may have views that are awful – but still lawful.
>
> It is equally critical to understand that every ideologically motivated extremist is not automatically a left-wing or right-wing extremist. There is a cohort of individuals motivated by a toxic cocktail of conspiracies, grievances and anti-authority beliefs. It is neither helpful nor accurate to reflexively assign these individuals to a place on the political spectrum.
>
> These are not simply semantic or academic distinctions. Words matter. Facts matter. Actions matter. If we, as a community, persist in getting the diagnosis wrong, we will struggle to find a cure.
>
> While threat to life will always be a priority for ASIO, espionage and foreign interference is now our principal security concern…

The rest of his address concerns foreign threats.

In 2021 ASIO changed its own domestic terrorism 'umbrella' categorisation to Religiously Motivated Violent Extremism, RMVE, and Ideologically Motivated Violent Extremism, IMVE. In this division the Trains sit with the al Qa'ida and ISIL groups. 'Right-wing extremism' was out, *verboten*. Aside from having a taste for theology and a record of blood-soaked deeds in common, the fit is very odd.

Counter-terrorism and extremist expert Lydia Khalil found the new terms vague, confusing, problematic and unfit for purpose; that is, identifying extremists and countering them. All extremists are ideological, even jihadis and the Trains. When South Australia Police announced they had raided lots of houses in Adelaide and arrested two men 'in relation to "ideologically motivated violent extremism"' and possession of an improvised explosive device, the nature of the extremists was a mystery until a well-known local neo-nazi complained to reporters it was members of his outfit whose houses were raided. As the National Socialist Network had previously confined themselves to burning a cross in the Grampians National Park, vandalism, assaults, insults and sticking racist graffiti on walls, building an IED was a quantum leap in the NSN's potential for causing death and destruction.

Khalil pointed out that Mike Burgess had been grilled up in parliamentary estimates committee hearings by Senator Concetta Fierravanti-Wells, a member of the Liberal Party's hard-right faction, concerned that ASIO's use of the word 'right' would offend many conservative Australians, causing them 'unwarranted and unnecessary angst'. In the US during the Trump years use of 'right-wing extremism' was similarly scrupulously avoided.[5]

Can the public can help law-enforcement officers track and curtail the activities, online and off, of potential terrorists with information? We know far-right extremists recruit and groom in prison gangs, outlaw motorcycle clubs, ex-military circles, trade and professional organisations, and teenagers' bedrooms, male's mainly. All these people have friends and relations who can help nip terrorism in the bud. Extremist groups are typically moving, name-changing, shape-shifting targets. But not calling a neo-Nazi a neo-Nazi (or eco-fascist, or whatever) is unhelpful. 'Words matter.'

The AFP's Acting Assistant Commissioner Counter Terrorism and

Special Investigations Sandra Booth has urged parents and guardians to be aware that extremist groups are using popular online games like Minecraft and Roblox to recruit the young. Her investigators used as an example one who engaged with extremist content – a recreation of the Christchurch mosque attacks – in a game and shared the content on his social media platforms.

Elsewhere, the AFP had before 2022 put far-right terrorism at 2 percent of their work in the area; it has hit 15 percent since.

* * *

Conspiracy-theorist recruiting and self-radicalising online can theoretically be policed online. It is suggested law enforcement could benefit from knowing what media posts the proto-extremist consulted, the hashtags used, content shared and, above all, the language they were using.

Right-leaning individuals tend to use moral language relating to vice (for example, harm, cheating, betrayal, subversion, and degradation), as opposed to virtue (care, fairness, loyalty, authority and sanctity), more than left-leaning individuals. Far-right individuals use grievance language (involving violence, hate and paranoia) significantly more than moderates.[6]

Thus, the detection of such signals of extremist ideology, could flag individuals and online communities for early investigation by law enforcement.

There are apps galore available that promise useful intelligence on open source and social media or both. For example, one claims the ability to track tweets and provide the physical location of a Twitter user. Tracing names, including hashtags and aliases, on, say, Facebook and LinkedIn can be the start of drawing up a complete footprint of a person or a site.

Profile images matched. Authorship analysis tools in extremist group's web forums. Web mining to collect and monitor. Natural language processing for detecting extremists on social media platforms. *Etcetera.*

It is easy in retrospect to highlight the flags of extremism in the known online input emanating from the Trains, but hard to imagine why an analyst would linger on anything they wrote even if some broad-sweep technique had turned their accounts up. For example, the words 'police' and 'kill' are not used. The totality of the data is vast. The number of police and intelligence technical analysts few. It may be true that capitalising the word CONTROL as Gareth was apt to do, is a flag to an experienced analyst of extremist language who read them, but how many of those readers are there, and how much time have they got? The Trains YouTube videos were not much viewed – low double digits until they killed – so tracing the Trains back from their suspicious connections would have been hugely unlikely. When do police step in and commit human or other resources when following a suspected extremist-in-the-making?

The AFP are recruiting such analysts and technical specialists.

The Queensland Police Service announced it was changing its procedures and will record online interactions with extremists on its state-wide database, Qprime. The QPS's idea of 'extremist' – they implied both far-right and far-left among the politically-motivated – hit objection straight away.'[7]

The area is a political, ethical, religious minefield.

The UK's two big problems, monitoring jihadists, Islamic State in particular, and curbing radicalisation and recruitment online have been under the umbrella of their Prevent strategy, launched with the passage of the Terrorist Act, since 2006.[8]

In May 2019 New Zealand PM Jacinda Ardern and France's president Emmanuel Macron formed the nucleus of the Christchurch Call.

Seminal in this initiative was the fact that the Christchurch mosque shooter's blood-soaked video was viewed over 4000 times before it was, very quickly, taken down. Ardern and Macron saw a global problem requiring global action, specifically heads of government and leaders in the technology sector. The Call seeks 'to eliminate terrorist & violent extremist content online'. Big call, 'eliminate'. They have now 58 member countries, including Australia, Indonesia, India and the US. Online service provider members include Amazon, Meta (Facebook, Instagram, What'sApp...), Google, Microsoft, Twitter and YouTube.

Police also train volunteers who make online presentations to parents, carers and teachers on keeping children online safer from the attentions of child abusers, the ThinkUKnow initiative. That could be expanded or copied to combat the recruiting or self-radicalisation of teenagers going down extremist rabbit holes.

The Living Safely Together has links to the National Security Hotline 1800 1234 00, Crime Stoppers and eSafety with trained operators to handle reports of 'any material that you've found on the internet that is violent extremist in nature or could encourage radicalisation towards violence'. Specifically:

- articles, images, speeches or videos that encourage hate or violence
- statements or posts made on social media, chat rooms or blogs that encourage hate or violence
- content encouraging people to commit acts of terrorism
- websites created or hosted by terrorist organisations
- terrorist training materials
- suspicious content regarding use or sale of chemicals online
- videos or images of terrorist attacks

The fight against hate and violence has been joined.

* * *

The idea the Wieambilla shootings was a *Christian* RMVE bought howls of rage from conservative Christian activists. Queensland Police spokeswoman Deputy Commissioner Tracy Linford and her colleagues were 'ignoramuses' and 'christophobes'. In a crack at Islam, 'Such a link would be easy to draw, as it is with false religions whose founder was a murdering war lord terrorist with a track record to back up his explicit incitements to violence'. In a crack at other enemies of conservative Christians, 'There is more basis for prepper terrorism in the climate alarmism dogma preached by leftists, globalists and elitists than such orthodox Christian doctrine as premillennialism, so why isn't the lying harlot media (LHM) blamed for this tragedy?'[9]

Mark Powell, minister at Strathfield NSW's Cornerstone Presbyterian Community Church (not that wishy-washy Uniting mob), found the cops to be woefully ignorant too. To call a belief in premillennialism 'extremist' was simply wrong. '… that Jesus is going to physically return to earth or that we are living in the last days is not "Christian extremist ideology".' It is 'traditional mainstream belief' he thundered under a photoshopped image of a man in with a shotgun looking at an ominous darkening sky.[10] Lyle Shelton, candidate for a seat in the NSW upper house and ex-CEO of the Australian Christian Lobby with the re-birthed Family First Party, agreed on Facebook.

All stressed that Christianity abhors violence and fired off some submit-to-authority Biblical quotations.

* * *

The wave of Islamic extremist terrorism that began in New York and Washington in 2001 killed over 100 Australians, 10 on that 9/11 day, 92 in two attacks in Indonesia, and a few – how many, arguable – on Australian soil. This takes no account of failed attempts to kill others, or, in the grim language of warfare, lives lost as 'collateral damage'. How many of us today remember the suicide car-bomb attack on the Australian Embassy in Jakarta in 2004 which killed nine people and injured 150 or so, none of them Australian? We have no way of counting how many Australians' or others' lives were saved by Operations Pendennis, Neath, Okra and Appleby.[11] But the stories and contexts, the work of police and intelligence organisations here, show Islamic extremists were thwarted before they became terrorists.

The wave of Far-Right extremist terrorism that began for us on 15 March 2019 with the mosque shootings in New Zealand, an attack which was originally planned to be on an Australian target, has already taken three Australian lives – those of Rachael, Matthew and Alan. I would argue that the Wieambilla killers absorbed enough from Far-Right extremist conspiracy theory for those tags to apply. I would argue the shooters' lack of nationalistic or racial elements, lack of affiliation to political organisations or cells, and disinterest in trying to influence the state, hallmarks of classic terrorism, are not sufficient departures for the charge of terrorism not to apply. Their bizarre religious motivations, I would argue, does not absolve them from a wish to terrorise, specifically, police officers.

Let us hope the Wieambilla murders are a close, not an incident in an on-going story. Hope as we may in counter-terrorism and national-security circles, right-wing extremism is only expected to grow. We have been warned.

1 Harry Clarke, *Country Caller*, 1 April 2023

2 Gerard Gill, 'Conspiracism, Extremism and the Battle over Sacred Values' GNET, 8 September 2021 – note the pre-Wieambilla shootings date – handles matters beyond the scope, coverage and aims of this book. Nevertheless, recommended reading.

3 Cam Wilson, 'Christian extremists belief that inspired the Wieambilla shooting a growing threat, experts say', *Crikey!* 17 February 2023

4 Paul Gregoire, *Sydney Criminal Lawyers*, 29 December 2022

5 Lydia Khalil, *Rise of the Extreme Right: the new global extremism and the threat to democracy*, 2022
6 Rohit Ram & Marian-Andrei Rizoiu, 'Can ideology-detecting algorithms catch online extremism before it takes hold?' *Conversation*, 27 February 2023
7 Miles Fitzsimmons, *People's World*, 31 March 2023 'Australian Police equate socialists with right-wing extremists, spy on both'
8 Erin Marie Sultan & Jonathan Russell, 'The Role of Prevent in Countering Online Extremism' (White Paper) 2 December 2014
9 Dave Pellowe, 'Police defame Christianity' *The Good Sauce*, 17 February 2023
10 'Was the Wieambilla Shooting an Act of Christian Terrorism?' *The Daily Declaration*, 20 February 2023
11 Kristy Campion, *Chasing Shadows: the untold story of terrorism in Australia*, 2022